knitted
sock
sensations

Louise Butt & Kirstie McLeod

knitted sock sensations

Over 40 fabulous looks for feelgood feet

Louise Butt & Kirstie McLeod

D&C

David and Charles

A DAVID & CHARLES BOOK
Copyright © David & Charles Limited 2008

David & Charles is an
F+W Publications Inc. company,
4700 East Galbraith Road
Cincinnati, OH 45236

First published in the UK and US in 2008

Text and designs copyright
© Louise Butt and Kirstie McLeod 2008
Photography and illustrations copyright
© David & Charles 2008

Louise Butt and Kirstie McLeod have asserted their
right to be identified as authors of this work in
accordance with the Copyright, Designs and
Patents Act, 1988.

A catalogue record for this book is available from
the British Library.

ISBN-13: 978-0-7153-2805-7 paperback
ISBN-10: 0-7153-2805-0 paperback

Printed in China by SNP Leefung
for David & Charles
Brunel House   Newton Abbot   Devon

Commissioning Editor Jennifer Fox-Proverbs
Desk Editor Bethany Dymond
Art Editor Sarah Underhill
Project Editor Nicola Hodgson
Production Controller Ros Napper
Photographer Lorna Yabsley

Visit our website at www.davidandcharles.co.uk

David & Charles books are available from all good
bookshops; alternatively you can contact our
Orderline on 0870 9908222 or write to us at
FREEPOST EX2 110, D&C Direct, Newton
Abbot, TQ12 4ZZ (no stamp required UK only);
US customers call 800-289-0963 and Canadian
customers call 800-840-5220.

Contents

Sock it to me!

Many knitters cherish an absolute passion for sock knitting. This might seem bewildering to the non-knitting world; after all, shop-bought socks are functional, forgettable items, easily overlooked and easily replaced when one goes astray in the wash. To the sock knitter, however, socks offer a glorious, colourful world of possibility, where crafty creativity meets wearable practicality. If you are a knitter who has yet to succumb to the seduction of socks, this is the book to get you hooked. It is packed full of tantalising projects to appeal to every type of knitter, and to every type of sock-wearer.

We've divided our fabulous footwear into four sections.

The Long and the Short of It is an excellent starting place if you're new to sock knitting. This section showcases projects that could be described as everyday-with-a-twist. We feature classic construction techniques, using both two-needle methods and knitting in the round on double-pointed needles. Each project, however, is a catalyst for creative inspiration. Try a straightforward tube sock, but make it in fresh, zingy colours (Around and Around Socks; pages 28–31). Or take a simple pattern, but knit it in a luxury colourful yarn and add a crocheted trim (Riding the Wave Socks; pages 50–53). And if you need any more convincing that sock knitting can be seductive, turn to pages 46–49; these stockings have tons of appeal!

Soothing the Sole is dedicated to blissfully cosy slipper socks. These are socks to wear around the house when you're in the mood for comfort, cosseting and warmth. There's a tempting array of projects to choose from; try the lush bedsocks in a luscious merino and angora yarn complete with a matching hot-water bottle cover (pages 74–79), or the bold, bright and beautiful ballerina slippers (pages 60–63). For the man in your life, we've got a pair of funky, furry gorilla feet (pages 70–73).

Tiny Tootsies features footwear for babies and children. Our projects include some kitschy-cute bootees for instant knitting gratification; choose from the tiger stripe, strawberry pip and ladybug spot versions (pages 82–85). A pair of delicately pretty fairy socks complete with embroidered embellishments (pages 90–93) would make a precious present; while the dashing pirate captain socks, complete with skull and crossbones (pages 98–99), will put children in the mood for adventure.

Think Outside the Socks will challenge your notions of what sock knitting can be. These fabulously quirky designs are fun, bold, stylish and eccentric. Try the split-toe socks (pages 116–119) or the stripy five-toe socks (pages 106–109) to transform your knitting from mundane to magical; conjure up some retro chic with the fabulous legwarmers (pages 110–115); and introduce some handmade charm to your Christmas, with the candy-stripe stocking and advent calendar mini-socks (pages 120–123).

Before we get to the projects, however, we start with an appetite-whetting section on the sorts of enticing yarns we've used for the designs (pages 8–11), and then go on to introduce the techniques required to make the patterns (pages 12–25). In the project notes we use a generic description of the yarn used, so you can easily substitute it. If you want to recreate the project exactly, we have listed the specific brands and shade numbers used on pages 126–127. We've also included a list of yarn suppliers (page 125).

Put your best foot forward and start sock knitting today!

Easy as one, two, three!

Whether you want a simple design to knit up in a hurry, or more of a challenge, you can quickly identify the difficulty of each pattern with this easy-to-follow guide:

  Simple

  Intermediate

  Advanced

Yarns your feet fantasize about

One of the joys of sock knitting is that we have a huge range of yarns to choose from, expanding our creative choices so that socks aren't just woolly, functional items but artworks for the feet. In this section we explore some of the options, including weight, yarn blends and texture.

Yarn weight

Most of the projects featured in this book use light-weight (DK) yarn, while some use medium-weight (aran) yarn. There are a few projects that use finer-weight yarn. If you get drawn into the world of sock knitting, as we hope you will, you'll find that a lot of dedicated sock yarns are fine-weight (4ply) or even lighter, and are often knitted up on needles ranging from about sizes 0 to 4 (2 to 3.5mm). These are beautiful yarns that produce a fine, light-weight sock, but they also take more time to knit, of course. We went for the slightly heavier-weight yarns as we wanted to emphasize quicker, more achievable projects that are fun to make, and that will inspire you to explore more.

The language of knitting

We have used US knitting terms for the projects in this book. If there are any terms you are unfamiliar with, refer to this box for a translation.

US term	UK term
bind off	cast off
gauge	tension
moss stitch	double moss stitch
seed stitch	moss stitch
stockinette stitch	stocking stitch
reverse stockinette stitch	reverse stocking stitch

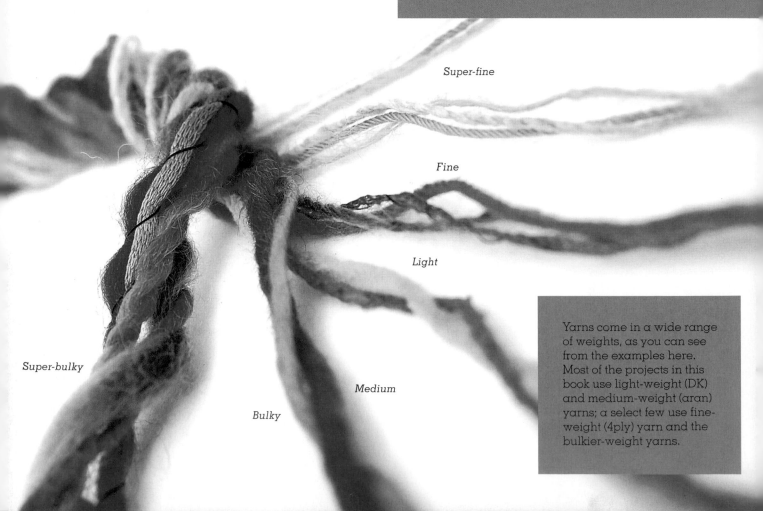

Super-fine

Fine

Light

Super-bulky

Medium

Bulky

Yarns come in a wide range of weights, as you can see from the examples here. Most of the projects in this book use light-weight (DK) and medium-weight (aran) yarns; a select few use fine-weight (4ply) yarn and the bulkier-weight yarns.

Light-weight (DK) yarn is in many ways an ideal weight of yarn for sock knitting. These yarns produce a soft knitted fabric that is comfortable to wear, fluid enough to mould to the shape of your foot, and fine enough to allow you to wear with your usual shoes. This weight of yarn is very versatile, and you'll find a huge number of brands and yarn blends available. Socks knitted in this weight of yarn are also fairly quick to knit, so you'll have the satisfaction of wearing something you've made before too long.

These socks with fancy cuffs are made in a light-weight (DK) yarn, so they produce a knitted fabric that is soft on your foot and thin enough to wear under shoes.

Medium-weight (aran) yarn has been our choice for some of the slipper socks and other projects for footwear that you probably wouldn't wear under shoes or boots. This weight of yarn makes a chunkier, warmer fabric that will be more hard-wearing, and therefore more suitable for footwear that you'll wear around the house.

These striking Swedish-style socks are knitted in a medium-weight (aran) yarn. They produce a pleasingly chunky, sturdy fabric that will really keep your feet warm.

merino and angora blend (pages 74–76)

bamboo and wool blend (pages 116–119)

acrylic pp 60–63

Yarns for sock knitting tend to be quite smooth and even in texture so that the sock is comfortable to wear against your skin. There is still a wide variety of yarns to choose from, however, as a large number of fibres, including wool, alpaca, cashmere, angora, bamboo, and a huge number of blended yarns are suitable.

These charming little bootees are knitted in a yarn that blends wool with acrylic and nylon. This combines the best qualities of each fibre: the wool adds warmth and softness to the fabric, while the synthetic fibres are hard-wearing and stable.

These socks are made from the poshest of fibres: pure cashmere. Cashmere is high-maintenance, but everyone deserves this level of indulgence sometimes.

Yarn types

Choose your sock yarn with care, as many types of yarn will not be suitable. The ideal sock yarn is one that produces a fabric with a fairly smooth, even and soft texture, so it is comfortable to wear against your skin. Yarns with a lot of texture, such as bouclé, astrakhan or slubbed yarns, could be less comfortable.

Sock yarn also needs to have a fair amount of 'give', or elasticity. Feet are a peculiar shape, with lots of knobbly bits, and the knitted fabric needs to be able to hug the shape of your foot without restricting it. For this reason yarns with no stretch, such as pure cotton, linen or silk, don't make good sock yarns.

Another important factor is the resilience of the yarn. Your socks will get a lot of wear and tear, and the fibre of the yarn needs to be able to withstand this. Something like a mohair yarn will be too wispy, while many ribbon yarns will be too fluid and sloppy. You'll also need to consider the aftercare of your sock. We tend to wear socks for a day and then put them in the laundry, so your sock yarn will need to put up with a lot of washing, whether by hand or by machine.

The yarn types that we've used could be put into five broad categories: luxury yarns, such as pure cashmere; luxury blends, such as merino and angora or alpaca and silk; pure wool; wool blended with synthetic fibres; and 100% synthetic yarn. Each of these yarn types has its merits. A luxury blend such as alpaca and silk produces a gloriously soft, lustrous and smooth fabric. Pure wool yarn is wonderfully warm and cosy. Acrylic yarn is economical, versatile and easy to look after, as it's hard-wearing and machine-washable.

These fantastically patterned legwarmers are made in pure wool, and will stave off the harshest of winter chills.

Standard yarn weight system

Confusion can sometimes arise with weights of yarn because there are several ways of describing the different categories, particularly in different parts of the world. In this book we have used US terms to describe the weights used, with the UK term in brackets. However, for a clearer idea on the categories of yarn that are in use in the UK and US, please refer to the table below – this is the Craft Yarn Council of America's standard yarn weight system.

Yarn Weight and Category Names	0 LACE	1 SUPER FINE	2 FINE	3 LIGHT	4 MEDIUM	5 BULKY	6 SUPER BULKY
TYPES OF YARNS IN CATEGORY	Fingering 10-count crochet thread	Sock, Fingering, Baby	Sport, Baby	DK, Light Worsted	Worsted, Afghan, Aran	Chunky, Craft, Rug	Bulky, Roving
KNIT GAUGE RANGE* IN STOCKINETTE STITCH TO 4 INCHES	30–40** sts	27–32 sts	23–26 sts	21–24 sts	16–20 sts	12–15 sts	6–11 sts
NEEDLE IN METRIC SIZE RANGE	1.25–1.5mm	2.25–3.25mm	3.25–3.75mm	3.75–4.5mm	4.5–5.5mm	5.5–8mm	8mm and larger
NEEDLE US SIZE RANGE	000–1	1–3	3–5	5–7	7–9	9–11	11 and larger
CROCHET GAUGE* RANGES IN SINGLE CROCHET TO 4 INCHES	32–42 double crochets**	21–32 sts	16–20 sts	12–17 sts	11–14 sts	8–11 sts	5–9 sts
HOOK IN METRIC SIZE RANGE	Steel*** 1.4–1.6mm	2.25–3.5mm	3.5–4.5mm	4.5–5.5mm	5.5–6.5mm	6.5–9mm	9mm and larger
HOOK US SIZE RANGE	Steel*** 6, 7, 8 Regular hook B1	B1 to E4	E4 to 7	7 to I9	I9 to K10½	K10½ to M13	M13 and larger

* GUIDELINES ONLY: The above reflect the most commonly used gauges and needle or hook sizes for specific yarn categories.

** Lace-weight yarns are usually knitted or crocheted on larger needles and hooks to create lacy, openwork patterns. Accordingly, a gauge range is difficult to determine. Always follow the gauge stated in your pattern.

*** Steel crochet hooks are sized differently from regular hooks – the higher the number, the smaller the hook, which is the reverse of regular hook sizing.

Casting on

Over the next few spreads we'll remind you of the basic knitting techniques that you will need to make socks, and also introduce you to some more specialist techniques that you might need. Let's start at the very beginning: casting on.

Knitting on

As experienced knitters know, there are many methods for casting on. For socks, however, you'll need a fairly loose cast-on row, and the knitting-on technique is ideal for this.

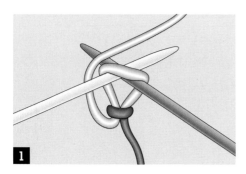

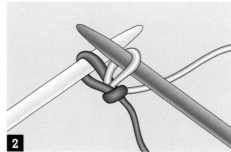

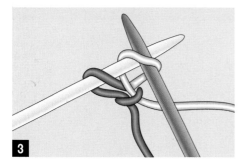

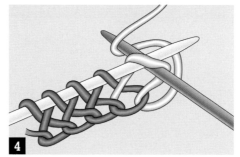

Make a slipknot in the working end of your yarn and place it on the left-hand needle. Insert your right needle into the loop of the slipknot and wrap the yarn around the tip of the needle, from back to front (1). Slide the tip of the right needle down to catch this new loop of yarn (2) and place the new loop on to the left-hand needle (3). This is your second stitch. Repeat this process until you have cast on as many stitches as you need (4).

Cable cast-on

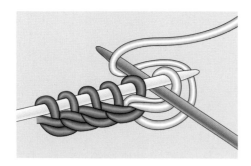

This is a useful method because you can use it to cast on stitches at the beginning of a row or in the middle of one. You might want to use it for the projects that have shaped toes (such as the Silky Split-Toe Socks, pages 116–119, or the Five-Toed Stripy Socks, pages 106–109), where you need to cast on stitches in mid-row or mid-round. This technique creates a firm and stable edge.

Using the knitting-on process described above, cast on two stitches. Then insert the right-hand needle *between* these two stitches. Wrap the yarn around the tip of the needle, from back to front, slide the needle down to catch the loop, and put this new loop on the left-hand needle. Repeat this process until you have as many stitches as you need.

Knit and purl stitches

Knit and purl stitches are the two basic knit stitches. Knowing just these two simple stitches will take you a very long way.

The knit stitch

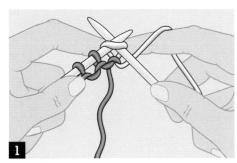

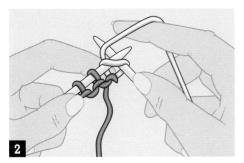

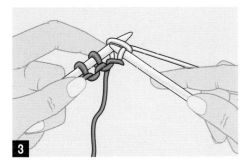

The working stitches will be on your left-hand needle. Take your right-hand needle and insert the tip from right to left into the first loop on the left-hand needle (1). Wrap the yarn from back to front around the tip of the right-hand needle (2). Slide the needle down to catch this new loop of yarn (3), and slip the loop off the left-hand needle. This is your first stitch. Repeat the process to the end of the row.

The purl stitch

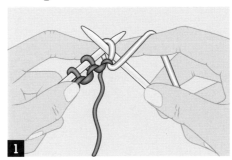

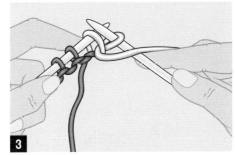

The working stitches will be on your left-hand needle. Take your right-hand needle and insert the tip from right to left through the front of the first loop on the left-hand needle (1). Wrap the yarn counterclockwise around the tip of the right-hand needle (2), and then use the tip of this needle to pick up the new loop of yarn (3). Slide the loop off the left-hand needle. This is your first stitch. Repeat the process to the end of the row.

Needle sizes

In this book, we've given US needle sizes first, with metric sizes in brackets. The table below gives you a comprehensive list of conversions should you need to refer to it at any time.

US	Metric
0	2mm
1	2.25mm
	2.5mm
2	2.75mm
	3mm
3	3.25mm
4	3.5mm
5	3.75mm
6	4mm
7	4.5mm
8	5mm
9	5.5mm
10	6mm
10½	6.5mm
	7mm
	7.5mm
11	8mm
13	9mm
15	10mm
17	12.75mm
19	15mm
35	19mm
	20mm

Increasing and decreasing

Sock knitting involves quite a lot of shaping so that your knitted fabric fits neatly to the intricate shape of your foot. Even the simplest project featured in this book, the Around and Around Socks (pages 28–31), requires you to decrease for the toes. Here we outline some of the most common techniques for increasing and decreasing.

Making increases

Most conventionally constructed socks won't require you to increase any stitches. However, some of the projects in this book require you to increase, for example, to shape the soles on slippers and bootees, and to shape the calves on the longer-length projects such as the Luscious Legwarmers (pages 110–115).

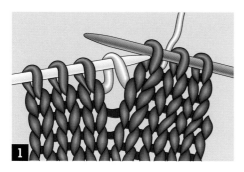
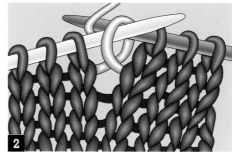

MAKE 1 (M 1)

To make this increase, you use the horizontal thread of yarn that lies between two stitches. When you have reached the point in your work where you need to make the increase, use the tip of the right-hand needle to lift up this horizontal strand and place it on the left-hand needle (1). You can then knit into the back of this loop as if it were a normal working stitch (2). Slip the new stitch off the left-hand needle, and your increase has been worked.

INCREASE 1 (INC 1)

This increase is also known as kfb (knit front and back). To make this increase, you knit into the front of the first loop on the left-hand needle as you would make a usual knit stitch (1). However, instead of slipping this stitch off the needle, you knit into the back of the stitch too, then slip the stitch onto the right-hand needle. This makes your new extra stitch.

This method of increasing can also be used on a purl row, in which case it may be described as pfb (purl front and back; 2). This form of increase is used to shape the soles of the Ballerina Bliss Slippers (pages 60–63), for example.

Making decreases

In conventional sock patterns, you are likely to decrease twice during the pattern: while working to shape the gusset, and when shaping the toe. You will often find that the decreases in sock patterns are paired together, so you have k2tog followed by ssk. Working increases in this way creates a neat finish to the item, as k2tog decreases slope to the right, and ssk to the left.

Increases and decreases are used to make curved and oval shapes, such as the soles of the Gorilla Feet Slippers (pages 70–73).

KNIT 2 TOGETHER (K2TOG)
To work this decrease, insert your right-hand needle first through the *second* stitch on your left-hand needle, and then through the first stitch. As usual, wrap the yarn round the tip of the right-hand needle, slide the needle down to pick up this new loop, and then slide both stitches off the left-hand needle.

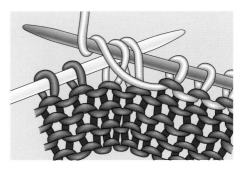

PURL 2 TOGETHER (P2TOG)
To work this decrease, insert your right-hand needle from right to left through the first two stitches on the left-hand needle. Wrap the yarn counterclockwise round the tip of the right-hand needle, pick this new loop off, and slide both stitches off the left-hand needle.

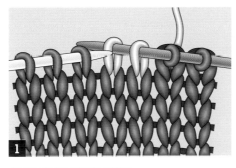

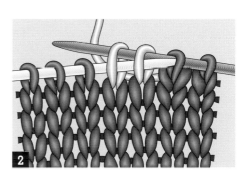

SLIP, SLIP, KNIT (SSK)
Insert the right-hand needle into the first stitch on the left-hand needle as if you were going to knit it, but simply slip it on to the right-hand needle. Do the same with the next stitch on the left-hand needle (1). Insert your left-hand needle through the fronts of these two stitches, from left to right. Then knit these two stitches together as one (2).

Further sock-knitting skills

A lot of the projects featured in this book use the traditional method of knitting socks; this means knitting in the round, using a set of four or five double-pointed needles. Another useful technique that you'll need to master is that of picking up stitches.

Using double-pointed needles

To knit many of the socks in this book you'll need to use a set of four double-pointed needles. The work is arranged evenly over three needles, with the fourth needle used as the working needle. (You might find it easier to arrange the work over four needles and use a fifth needle to work with when you have a particularly large number of live stitches – for example once you've picked up stitches to form the gusset.) Working in this way forms a seamless 'tube' of knitting.

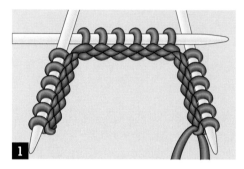

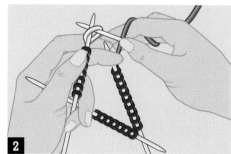

You'll start by casting on the number of stitches required onto one needle. Use the knitting-on method (see page 12), as your cast-on stitches will need to be fairly loose. When all the stitches have been cast on, divide the stitches evenly between three needles. Take a spare needle, slip the first group of stitches off knitwise onto this needle, and then repeat with a second needle. The last group of stitches stays on the needle on which they were originally cast on (1).

Now bring your needles together to form a triangle. It's helpful to mark the beginning of the round, so you could place a stitch marker here before you knit the first stitch. Bring your fourth needle into play, and knit the first stitch to form the round (2). You'll need to pull this stitch quite tight, or a noticeable gap or ladder will appear in the knitted fabric.

When you work in the round, you knit every round to form stockinette stitch – there's no need to turn the work and purl. The first few rows are often tricky and feel awkward, so work slowly and carefully. Make sure when you start the first row that all your stitches are facing inwards; otherwise it's possible to twist the stitches. Once you have knitted all the stitches off the first needle on to your working needle, this needle is free of stitches and in turn becomes your working needle.

The other thing to note about sock knitting is that you most often work from the cuff down to the heel. This means you're essentially knitting upside-down, which you might find odd if you're more used to knitting garments from the bottom up.

Many of the projects in this book are knitted in the round using double-pointed needles, including the Peppermint Pompom socks (pages 44–45). Knitting in the round creates a seamless item that is comfortable to wear.

Picking up stitches

When you knit socks in the round, you will need to pick up stitches. This occurs after you have knitted the heel flap and shaped the heel. You pick up stitches from the edges of the heel flap to form the gusset and to resume knitting in the round. You also pick up stitches to form the cuff of the Swedish Felted Slippers (pages 64–67).

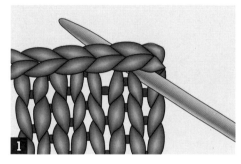

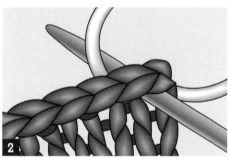

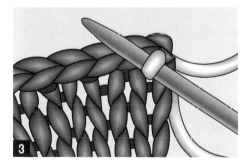

Hold the work in your left hand, and pick up stitches with the right hand needle. Insert the right-hand needle through both strands of the first stitch (1). Wrap the yarn round the tip of the right-hand needle as if you were knitting the stitch (2). Use the needle tip to draw the loop through the work (3). This is the first picked-up stitch; repeat until you have the number of stitches required.

Abbreviations

Knitting patterns generally use abbreviations to save on space and avoid repetition of instructions. Below you will find a list of the abbreviations that we have used in the projects for this book.

alt	alternate	**k2tog tbl**	knit 2 sts together through the back loop (decrease by 1 st)
beg	beginning (of row or round)	**kfb**	knit into front and back of stitch (increase by 1 st)
C2b	sl 1 st onto cable needle and hold at back, k1, p st from cable needle	**m1**	make 1 st by picking up the loop between 2 sts and placing it on left-hand needle, then work into the back of it (increase by 1 st)
C2B	sl 1 st onto cable needle and hold at back, k1, k st from cable needle		
C2f	sl 1 st onto cable needle and hold at front, p1, k st from cable needle	**p**	purl
		p2tog	purl 2 sts together (decrease by 1 st)
C2F	sl 1 st onto cable needle and hold at front, k1, k st from cable needle	**p2tog tbl**	purl 2 sts together through the back loop (decrease by 1 st)
C3b	sl 1 st onto cable needle and hold at back, k2, p st from cable needle	**patt**	pattern
C3f	sl 1 st onto cable needle and hold at front, p1, k2 sts from cable needle	**pfb**	purl into front and back of stitch (increase by 1 st)
C4B	place next 2 sts on cable needle and hold at back, k2, then k sts on cable needle	**pm**	place marker
		psso	pass the slipped stitch over
C4F	place next 2 sts on cable needle and hold at front, k2, then k sts on cable needle	**rem**	remain(ing)
		rep	repeat
		rev st st	reverse stockinette stitch
ch	chain (crochet stitch)	**sc**	single crochet
		sl	slip
cont	continue	**sl st**	slip stitch (crochet stitch)
dec	decrease		
dpn	double-pointed needle	**ssk**	slip, slip, knit (decrease by 1 st)
hdc	half double crochet	**st(s)**	stitch(es)
		st st	stockinette stitch
		tbl	through back of loop (a)
inc	increase	**yb**	yarn back
k	knit	**yf**	yarn forward
k2tog	knit 2 sts together (decrease by 1 st)	**yo (or yon)**	yarnover

Further decorative techniques

We use a lot of ways of sassing up our designs, from hand-sewn embellishments to using variegated yarns to create beautiful colour effects. We also explore some advanced knitting techniques to liven up the designs and make them really special. The principal two techniques we're using are cables and intarsia.

Intarsia

Intarsia is a way of introducing colourwork into your knitting. It involves using two or more colours of yarn in one row of knitting to make up an overall colour design. The design can be simple, such as the vertical stripes of the Two-Stripe Two-Needle Socks (pages 32–33), or more complex designs for which you follow a chart. The pattern of the Tiger Feet bootees (pages 82–84) and the fairies on the Fairy Socks (pages 90–93) are worked in this way.

To work intarsia designs you need to prepare a bobbin of yarn for each colour change. If you tried to work with a full skein of yarn you would probably end up in a hopeless mess. Even working with bobbins you will probably end up with a lot of loose yarn ends hanging at the back of the work, so it's usually best to darn them in as you go along to avoid them becoming tangled with your working yarns.

You can buy ready-made plastic bobbins to wind the yarn onto, or you can make your own by winding the yarn around your thumb and little finger in a figure of eight.

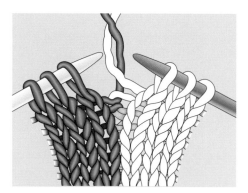

Whenever you change colours, you will need to twist the old and the new yarns together. Otherwise you will end up with ugly gaps or holes in the knitted fabric.

The places where you change yarn will show on the wrong side of the fabric, but at the front of the work the colour change, will be crisp and precise. The great thing about using intarsia for sock designs, of course, is that the scrappy colour changes and woven-in ends will be hidden from view on the inside of the sock.

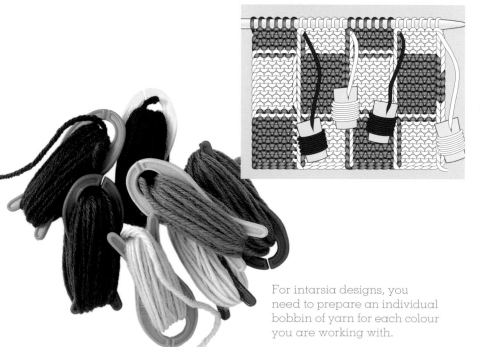

For intarsia designs, you need to prepare an individual bobbin of yarn for each colour you are working with.

Cables

Cables are a very traditional way of introducing textured patterns into your knitting; some cable designs originated centuries ago. We've used cables in two of our projects, the Celtic Cable socks (pages 40–43), and the Loveheart Legwarmers (pages 110–113), both of which show that this traditional technique has much to offer the contemporary knitter.

Knitting cables involves making a 'twist' in the knitted fabric. You do this by working stitches from a cable needle held either at the front (for a left cross) or the back (for a right cross) of the work. You can use either a short, straight double-pointed needle, or a special cable needle that has a 'kink' in it to hold the stitches on. There are many, many cable designs, but here we've demonstrated the basic technique using Cable Four Front (C4F) and Cable Four Back (C4B).

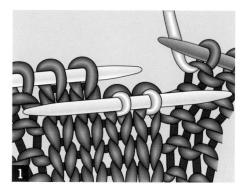 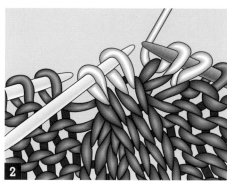

CABLE FOUR FRONT (C4F)

Work to the point where the cable twist is to be made. Slip the first two stitches on the left-hand needle onto your cable needle. Leave the cable needle hanging at the front of the work (1).

Knit the next two stitches on the left-hand needle, using the right-hand needle as usual. Then knit the two stitches held on the cable needle (2). Put the cable needle aside and knit the rest of the row as usual.

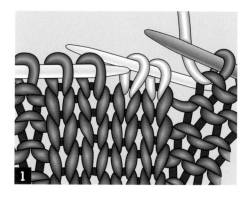 

CABLE FOUR BACK (C4B)

Work to the point where the cable twist is to be made. Slip the first two stitches on the left-hand needle onto your cable needle. Leave the cable needle hanging at the back of the work (1).

Knit the next two stitches on the left-hand needle, using the right-hand needle as usual. Then knit the two stitches held on the cable needle (2). Put the cable needle aside and knit the rest of the row as usual.

Knitted cables create complex and intricate patterns that stand out against the background of the knitted fabric.

Finishing off

On these pages we cover the techniques for finishing your socks, including binding off, joining the toe seam, and seaming.

Binding off

Any of the designs that are knitted straight on two needles will need to be bound off in the usual way.

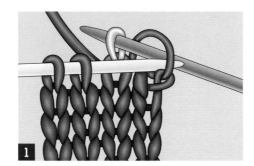

To bind off, you work the first stitch off the left-hand needle as if making a usual knit stitch (see page 13). Then knit the second stitch. Insert your left-hand needle into the first stitch on the right-hand needle (1). Then pass this over the second loop on the right-hand needle, and drop it off the needle (2). This is the first bound-off stitch. Knit the next stitch, and again, use your left-hand needle to pass the first stitch over the second stitch and drop it off the needle. Continue in this way until all the stitches in the row have been bound off.

Joining the toe seam

One of the main advantages of making socks in the round is that the whole body of the sock is made in one continuous tubular piece. This means that the only seam to join is at the toe. This is a boon to the many knitters who much prefer knitting to sewing! In the projects, we suggest joining the toe with one of two methods: using a three-needle bind-off, or grafting. Both of these techniques create a seamless join on the outside of the sock.

THREE-NEEDLE BIND-OFF

The three-needle bind-off creates a seamless join on the outside of the sock, but will create a ridge of bound-off stitches on the inside. You will need to carefully turn the work inside-out so that the knit side of the stockinette fabric is inside and the purl side is facing you (you might want to put the live stitches on small safety pins to do this).

Divide the remaining stitches evenly between two needles, one needle holding the stitches for the top part of the foot and the other holding stitches for the underneath of the toe. Hold the two needles together in your left hand and, using a third needle, insert this through the first stitches on both left-hand needles. Knit the stitches together. Repeat this for the second two stitches on the left-hand needle. When you have two stitches on the right-hand needle, you can bind off in the usual way (see above). Repeat this process until all the stitches are bound off, and tie off the yarn.

Grafting creates a seamless and invisible join at the toe.

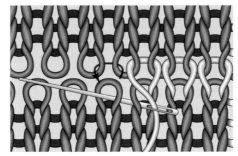

GRAFTING

Grafting is a way of sewing the toe stitches together in a way that imitates a knitted row of stitches. This technique is also known as kitchener stitch. This method creates a join that is invisible and seamless on both the right side and wrong side of the knitted fabric.

Again, you will need to divide the remaining stitches evenly between two needles, one holding stitches for the top of the foot and the other holding stitches for the under part of the foot.

You'll use the yarn coming from the last stitch that you knitted. Cut the yarn, leaving about 30cm (12in) to graft the stitches with. Thread the yarn onto a darning needle.

Insert the needle purlwise into the first stitch on the front needle and pull the yarn through. Insert the needle knitwise into the first stitch on the back needle and pull the yarn through.

*Insert the needle knitwise into the first stitch on the front needle and slip the stitch off the needle. Insert the needle purlwise into the next stitch on the front needle and pull the yarn through. Insert the needle purlwise into the first stitch on the back needle and slip this stitch off the needle. Insert the needle knitwise into the next stitch on the back needle and pull the yarn through. Repeat from * to * until all the stitches have been grafted. Darn in the loose end.

Seaming with mattress stitch

This technique is for joining pieces made straight on two needles. This method makes an invisible seam when joining two pieces of stockinette fabric, or when seaming one piece of stockinette fabric into a tube, as you'll most commonly be doing when seaming socks that have been made on two needles.

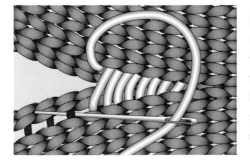

Place the pieces to be joined with the right side facing you. You'll work the seam from bottom to top, stitching around the horizontal bars that run like a ladder between the Vs of stockinette stitch (you'll see these if you gently pull a piece of stockinette fabric apart).

Thread a darning needle with the length of yarn you're using for the seam (ideally this will be the same yarn you used to knit the piece). Pass the needle under the first two running bars of the right-hand piece of fabric, from the bottom to the top. Then pass the needle under the first two running bars of the left-hand piece of fabric. Insert the needle down into the point where it came out on the right-hand piece of fabric, and carry it under the next two running bars on the right-hand side. Insert the needle back into the same point where it came out on the left-hand piece of fabric, and carry it under the next two running bars on the left-hand side. When you have repeated this process a few times, pull the yarn taut (but not too tightly, or the seam will pucker) so the seam becomes invisible. Carry on in this way until the whole piece has been seamed together.

Embellishments

We hope to inspire you with the variety of ways that you can embellish your designs once your project is knitted and made up. Some of these include stitching on beads, buttons, and other ready-made items to beautify your socks, as with the Short and Sweet Sockettes (pages 54–57) and the Fairy Socks (pages 90–93). We're also suggesting adding embroidery and handmade pompoms. These techniques are described in more detail below.

Embroidery

Hand-embroidering designs onto a sock or slipper is a lovely way of making them unique and beautiful. Choose an embroidery yarn that will really stand out against the knitted fabric.

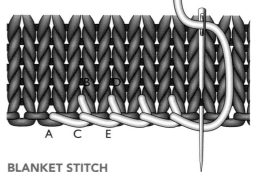

BLANKET STITCH

Blanket stitch is a bold-looking stitch ideal for embellishing the edge of an item, which is how we've used it on the Swedish Felted Slippers (pages 64–67).

Thread your needle with the contrast-colour yarn. Bring the needle out at A, and then, in one movement, take it down at B and back up at C, looping the thread under the needle tip. You work the next stitch to the right, taking the needle down at D and up at E. The horizontal threads of the stitches should lie right at the edge of the knitted piece.

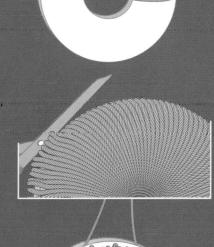

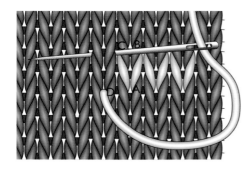

SWISS DARNING

Swiss darning is a way of adding small colour details to knitted work. It is also known as duplicate stitch, as you sew straight over the knitted stitch so the sewn stitch looks as though it were part of the knitted fabric.

To swiss darn over stockinette stitch, first thread an embroidery needle with yarn the same thickness as the yarn used for the knitted fabric. Bring the needle out of the work at the base of the stitch, A. Then in one movement, take the yarn around the top of the stitch by taking the needle down at B and up at C. Again in one movement, take the needle down at the base of the stitch (A) and up at the base of the next stitch (D).

The strawberry 'pips' on these bootees have been created by swiss darning.

Pompoms

You can buy ready-made pompoms, but it's easy and fun to make your own, especially if you want to make them in a specific yarn to complement a hand-knitted item.

To make a pompom 1½in (4.5cm) in diameter, you need to cut out two fairly sturdy cardboard discs that also have a diameter of 1½in (4.5cm). This is roughly the size of a pepper mill or spice pot, so you could use one of those to draw round to create your template. You then need to cut out discs in the centre of the circles – about half the size of the original circles. (If you only have scissors rather than a craft knife, you can cut through the outside edge of the cardboard to get to the inner circle, cut out the inner circle, and then sellotape the cut sides together to keep the disc together.) Your cardboard discs should now look like flat doughnuts.

Hold your discs together, and start wrapping yarn around the 'doughnut' ring. The whole ring needs to be completely covered – you shouldn't be able to see any of the cardboard underneath, and the hole in the centre should be completely filled. Towards the end, you may find it helpful to thread yarn on to a tapestry needle. This will give you a good full, round pompom.

When the wrapping is complete, you need to cut through all the loops of yarn, working your way round the outside edge of the doughnut. Once this is done, take a longer piece of yarn, slip it between the two cardboard rings, pull it tight (very tight) around the core of the pompom and tie a secure knot in it. You can now cut the cardboard rings out. Your pompom is done! You might need to trim off some yarn ends to make it even, and plump it up a bit to make it nice and round.

Crochet

A lot of knitters regard crochet with fear and suspicion, but crochet is a simple technique to learn and a lovely way to add design flourishes to knitted items. We use crochet trims and embellishments on several projects, including the Riding the Wave Socks (pages 50–53), the Ballerina Bliss Slippers (pages 60–63) and the Silky Split-Toe Socks (pages 116–119). The trim for these first two projects is worked around the edge of the knitted cuff, while the embellishments for the split-toe socks are made independently and then stitched into place.

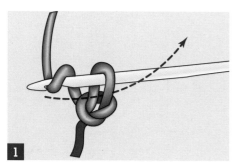

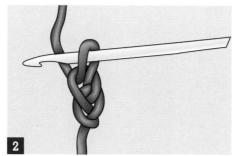

Chain (ch)

For the Silky Split-Toe embellishments, you need to start off by crocheting a chain to act as your foundation row.

First tie a slipknot in the working end of your yarn and place the loop on the crochet hook. Wrap the yarn clockwise over the hook (1), then pull the yarn through the loop on the hook to form a fresh loop (2). This counts as one chain stitch. Repeat the process until you have as many chain stitches as you need.

Joining the chain into a circle

When you're making the Silky Split-Toe embellishments, the next stage is to join your chain into a circle. To do this, insert your hook into the first chain stitch, wrap the yarn clockwise around your hook, and then pull the yarn through both the first chain and the loop of the last chain of the row (that is, the loop that is already on the hook). This joins the circle.

Crochet conversions

You should be aware that crochet terms in the US are different from those in the UK. This can be particularly confusing as the same terms are used to refer to different stitches under each system. We use US terms only in the pattern instructions in this book. Refer to the list below for a translation.

US term	UK term
slip stitch	single crochet
single crochet	double crochet
half double crochet	half treble
double crochet	treble
treble crochet	double treble
double treble crochet	treble treble

The decorations for the Silky Split-Toe Socks are simple to crochet; make a chain, join into a circle, and work a row of single crochet stitches.

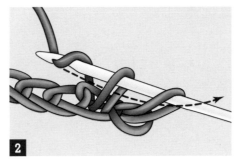

Single crochet (sc)

The single crochet stitch is the shortest of the crochet stitches. To make the stitch, insert your hook under the top two strands of the stitch beneath (or, if you're working into the foundation row, insert the hook into the centre of the chain stitch). Wrap the yarn over the hook and pull the yarn through (1). Then wrap the yarn over the hook again and pull it through both the loops on the hook (2). This forms one single crochet stitch.

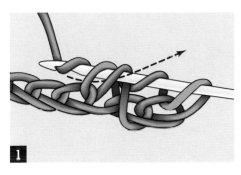

Half double crochet (hdc)

The half double crochet stitch is slightly taller than the single crochet stitch. To make the stitch, wrap the yarn over the hook and then insert it under the top two strands of the stitch beneath (or, if you're working into the foundation row, insert the hook into the centre of the chain stitch). Wrap the yarn over again, and pull it through the work (1). You will now have three loops of yarn sitting on the hook. Wrap the yarn over again and pull it through all three loops on the hook (2). This is one half double crochet stitch.

It's quite simple to work crochet stitches around the top of a knitted piece, as you'll be doing for the Riding the Wave Socks (pages 50–53) and the Ballerina Bliss Slippers (pages 60–63). Decide where you're going to start the crochet round. Insert the crochet hook underneath both the horizontal strands of yarn at the top of one knitted stitch. Make a slipknot in the working end of your yarn, and place the loop of the slipknot onto your crochet hook. Pull this loop through the knitted fabric (this action is very similar to that used for picking up stitches; see page 17). You can now start your crochet work.

The long and the short of it...

First step tube socks

The two projects in this section are perfect for first-time sock knitters because there's no heel to turn. These funky tube socks have no shaping until the simple decreases for the toe. The support around the heel comes from the simple ribbed pattern that creates elasticity, hugging the contours of your foot. If you're new to sock knitting, have a go with the two-needle pattern; you can then progress and make the other socks using the four-needle method. Our versions are knee-length, but you can make them any length you like. Just stop when you've had enough!

Around and around

 Simple

These socks are a great project if you've never knitted in the round before with double-pointed needles. As the name suggests, they are worked straight to form a tube, so you'll have plenty of time to get used to working with a handful of needles! To liven up your learning process, work your socks in some funky, eye-popping colours, as brash and bright as you like.

Once you've got the hang of knitting in the round, you can start working some colour magic to make this simple pattern that much more fun to knit – and to wear.

Measurements

To fit three calf widths:
Small [Medium: Large]
Overall length of sock is 20½in (53cm) but can be worked longer or shorter

Gather together...

MATERIALS
Light-weight (DK) wool, acrylic and nylon mix yarn (see individual instructions for colour details)

NEEDLES AND NOTIONS
1 set of size 1 (2.5mm) double-pointed needles
1 set of size 4 (3.5mm) double-pointed needles
Stitch marker

Gauge

Achieving an exact gauge is not essential for this project because the ribbing makes the knitted fabric stretchy

There's no shaping at all in these tube socks until you decrease for the toe – instead, the stretchy ribbing will mould to the contours of your foot.

Raspberry ribbing

If you are a beginner to socks, start off using one bold colour, such as the vivid red version shown opposite.

MATERIALS
2 x 1¾oz (50g) balls in red
Work the basic pattern using the red yarn throughout.

Knit your socks...

(Make 2)
Cast on 45 [51: 57] sts using size 1 (2.5mm) double-pointed needles.
Evenly distribute sts over 3 needles and place marker to indicate the beginning of the round. Now work in the round, taking care not to twist sts.
Round 1 (K2, p1) to end of round.
Cont as set until knitting measures 1in (2.5cm).
Change to size 4 (3.5mm) double-pointed needles.
Cont in pattern until sock measures 19in (48cm).

SHAPE TOE
* Change to size 1 (2.5mm) double-pointed needles.
Work 3 rounds in pattern.
Next round (K2tog, p1) to end of round.
Work 3 more rounds.
Next round K2tog to end of round.
K 1 round.
Transfer sts to 2 dpns and graft rem sts (see page 21). Darn in any loose ends.

Lemon 'n' lime

Stripes are a simple but sassy way to introduce lively colour (see opposite). We worked thick stripes of contrasting lemon and lime for a fresh, summery look.

Tutti frutti bands

We worked four wide bands of colour around the calf, and four narrower bands at the toe (see image on previous page).

MATERIALS
A 1 x 1¾oz (50g) ball in purple
B 1 x 1¾oz (50g) ball in red
C 1 x 1¾oz (50g) ball in pink
D 1 x 1¾oz (50g) ball in yellow

Knit your socks...

(Make 2)
Cast on as for Raspberry Ribbing in yarn A.
Work 1in (2.5cm) in rib patt.
Change needle size.
Work 8 rounds in yarn B, 8 rounds in yarn C, 8 rounds in yarn D. Then change to yarn A and cont until work measures 17½in (44cm).
Work 4 rows in yarn B, 4 rows in yarn C, and 4 rows in yarn D.
Now change to yarn A and work toe as from *.

MATERIALS
1 x 1¾oz (50g) ball in green
1 x 1¾oz (50g) ball in yellow
Work the basic pattern, swapping yarn colours every 1½in (4cm).

Just because your socks are long, doesn't mean you're short on looks. Turn them over, scrunch them down, or wear them high with pride. It's up to you!

tip

Ensure that each needle ends on 2 knit stitches of the rib, so that ladders are not evident in the knitted fabric.

Two-stripe two-needle socks

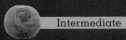

Intermediate

If you've never knitted a sock before and find four needles fiddly, then try this two-needle version of the simple tube sock. Again, the rib pattern will make the sock form well to your feet, ensuring the fit fits beautifully without the headache of turning the heel. We've made these nifty knee-highs with no toe shapes in fiery colours for some extra sass. You will need to work these stripes using the intarsia technique (see page 18). Wind the yarn onto individual bobbins before you start (see tip).

Measurements

One size fits all; overall length is 18in (46cm)

Gather together...

MATERIALS

A 1 x 1¾oz (50g) ball in light-weight (DK) wool, acrylic and nylon mix yarn in red

B 1 x 3½oz (100g) ball of light-weight (DK) acrylic yarn in orange

NEEDLES AND NOTIONS

1 pair of size 1 (2.5mm) needles
1 pair of size 4 (3.5mm) needles
2 size 1 (2.5mm) double-pointed needles for grafting

Gauge

Achieving an exact gauge is not essential for this project because the ribbing makes the knitted fabric stretchy

Knit your socks...

(Make 2)

Cast on 50 sts using size 1 (2.5mm) needles and yarn A.

Row 1 (RS) Set up rib patt: k1, (k2, p1) to last st, k1.

Row 2 P1, (k1, p2) to last st, p1.

Cont in rib patt as set until work measures 1in (2.5cm).

Change to size 4 (3.5mm) needles.

Next row Work 7 sts in patt, *join in yarn B and work 6 sts in patt, join in yarn A and work 6 sts in patt, rep from * twice more, join yarn B and work 7 sts.

Cont in stripe pattern for 16in (41cm) or desired length, ending on a right-side row.

SHAPE TOE

Change to size 1 (2.5mm) needles and work 3 rows using just yarn A.

Next row K1, (p2tog, k1) to last st, k1. 34 sts.

Next row K1, (k2tog) to last st, k1. 18 sts.

Place 9 middle sts onto size 1 (2.5mm) dpn and place rem sts onto another dpn.

Join the seam using mattress stitch (see page 21) on the right side of the sock. A 1 st allowance has been included to allow for this. Now graft the toe (see page 21). Darn in any loose ends.

The toe seam for these socks is joined together using grafting (see page 21).

If you use a bobbin or separate ball for each stripe colour, the wrong side (above) of your sock will look very neat. If we had used the Fair Isle method, there would be lots of loops where the yarn had carried.

tip

With these vertical-stripe socks, it's a good idea to wind your yarn onto separate bobbins, one for each colour (so that's three bobbins of each colour). Doing this means that you won't be carrying the yarn across the back of the work, which would cause rucking and prevent the elasticity of the rib effect. When you come to add each colour, just tie it to the working yarn and start knitting the next 6 stitches. You can darn in all loose ends securely once you've finished. When changing colour along the row, make sure that you twist the two yarns that are meeting together to prevent holes appearing in your work.

The easiest way of making stripes in knitting is to work horizontal bands of colour, changing the yarn at the ends of rows as necessary. Vertical stripes are a little trickier to achieve, as you need to use intarsia (see page 18), but the results can be stunning. Light up your life by using bold, hot colours as we have for this pair, or go monochrome with classic black and white.

Off the cuff socks

One of the fabulous things about knitting socks is the thousands of ways you can take a basic pattern and give it extra sass with quirky twists and colourful variations. Here, we've given three novel ideas for wild and woolly cuffs. Each cuff is knitted on straight needles; the work is then transferred to double-pointed needles, and the main part of the sock worked in the round with a properly turned heel. The socks are worked in standard light-weight (DK) yarn, so you'll have a huge range of yarns to choose from.

All in jest and Going loopy socks

These two variations are worked in one type of yarn to the same basic pattern. Going Loopy features a shaggy, bubbly, loop-stitch trim. This stitch is quite slow work, but it's worth the effort. All in Jest features a two-tone triangular trim reminiscent of court jesters' outfits, complete with a contrast-colour toe.

 Simple

Measurements

Small: foot at widest point 8¼in (21cm)

Medium: foot at widest point 9in (23cm)

Large: foot at widest point 10in (25cm)

Gather together…

MATERIALS
Light-weight (DK) wool, acrylic and nylon mix yarn

All in jest:
A 2 [2: 3] x 1¾oz (50g) balls in blue
B 1 [1: 1] x 1¾oz (50g) ball in pink

Going loopy:
2 [2: 3] x 1¾oz (50g) balls in pink

NEEDLES AND NOTIONS
1 pair of size 4 (3.5mm) needles
1 set of size 4 (3.5mm) double-pointed needles
Stitch marker

Gauge

19 sts and 27 rows to 4in (10cm) square measured over st st using size 4 (3.5mm) needles

Both versions of these socks feature a flamboyant fold-down trim. Concealed under the trim is a section of ribbing, which will help to hold the sock in place around your ankle.

Here the colourful cuff is worked in garter stitch. You work the first triangle, and then switch to the other colour of yarn, leaving the first triangle on your working needle. Once all eight triangles have been knitted you work across the whole row in one colour.

These socks feature a fully worked heel. You knit the heel flap first, back and forth on two double-pointed needles, then shape the heel, and then pick up stitches for the gusset.

tip

Here, you keep track of the gusset shaping decreases by referring to which needle they are on. You could also track this by placing a stitch marker on each side of the sock; on the right side you knit to 3 stitches before the marker, k2tog, k1, and on the left side you knit to the marker, k1, ssk.

Knit your All in jest cuff...
(Make 2)

(Cuff the same for all sizes)
Starting with yarn A, cast on 1 st using size 4 (3.5mm) straight needles.
Row 1 K.
Row 2 Kfb. 2 sts.
Row 3 K.
Row 4 K1, m1, k1. 3 sts.
Row 5 K.
Row 6 K1, kfb, k1. 4 sts.
Row 7 K.
Row 8 K1, m1, k2, m1, k1. 6 sts.
Row 9 K.
Leave sts on needle then rep with yarn B. Cont to rep triangle pattern until you have a total of 8 triangles on 1 needle.

Now K across all 48 sts with yarn B.
Knit 5 further rows in yarn B.
K 6 rows in yarn A.
Now evenly distribute the sts onto 3 size 4 (3.5mm) double-pointed needles, placing a marker to show the start of the round. Join and begin working in the round. Work a k2, p2 rib for 1in (2.5cm).

Next round Dec 4 sts evenly in round if making the smaller size; inc 4 sts if working largest size (no change necessary for middle size). 44 [48: 52] sts.
Cont as for Basic Sock (see page 38), but changing yarn colour to yarn B at the toe.

Special instruction

Loop st: Knit into st but do not drop the loop off the left-hand needle. Bring yarn forward between the two needles and wind it around the top of your left thumb. Take yarn back through the needles and k the st again, this time letting the loop on the left-hand needle drop. Now pass the 1st st over the 2nd. Rep this all across the row.

Loop stitch is quite time-consuming, as you have to wrap the yarn around your thumb to make each stitch. The effect is fabulous though, resulting in this curly, strokable fabric, somewhat like a shaggy rug.

The yarn for these socks is a mixture of wool and synthetic fibres; the wool adds warmth to the fibre mix, while the synthetic fibres are resilient and hard-wearing.

Knit your Going loopy cuff…

(Make 2)

Cast on 48 sts using size 4 (3.5mm) straight needles.

Row 1 K into the back of every stitch (this will create a good, firm foundation row).

Row 2 P.

Row 3 Loop st into every st.

Rep rows 2 and 3 a further 3 times.

Now evenly distribute the sts onto 3 size 4 (3.5mm) double-pointed needles, placing a marker to show the start of the round. Join and begin working in the round. Work a k2, p2 rib for 1in (2.5cm).

Next round Dec 4 sts evenly in round if making smaller size; inc 4 sts if working the largest size (no change necessary for middle size). 44 [48: 52] sts.
Cont as for Basic Sock (see page 38).

Knit your basic sock...

Starting from base of cuff: K every round for 1in (2.5cm) ending at marker.

HEEL FLAP

Divide sts between 2 needles so that there are 22 [24: 26] sts on each needle. You will work on just 1 needle; the other sts will form the gusset later on. When you turn your knitting you should be ready to start on a P row. You will work backwards and forwards in st st for the flap.

Row 1 Sl first st and p across row.
Next row Sl first st and k across row.
Rep last 2 rows 10 [11: 12] times more – 22 [24: 26] rows in total.
Next row Sl first st and p across row.

SHAPE HEEL

Sl 1, k13 [15: 16], ssk, turn.
Sl 1, p6 [8: 8] sts, p2tog, turn.
Sl 1, k6 [8: 8] sts, ssk, turn.
Rep last 2 rows until 8 [10: 12] sts rem, ending on a p row.

GUSSET

Now it's time to pick up sts.
With spare needle, k4 [5: 6] sts from heel needle.
Needle 1 K next 4 [5: 6] sts, then pick up and knit 13 [14: 15] sts from side of heel.
Needle 2 K across all 22 [24: 26] sts.
Needle 3 Pick up and knit 13 [14: 15] sts from side of heel and k across 4 [5: 6] sts on spare needle. 56 [62: 68] sts.

SHAPE GUSSET

Round 1
Needle 1 K to last 3 sts, k2tog, k1.
Needle 2 K.
Needle 3 K1, ssk, k to end of needle.

Round 2
K all 3 needles.

Rep last 2 rounds until:
Needle 1 11 [12: 13] sts rem.
Needle 2 22 [24: 26] sts.
Needle 3 11 [12: 13] sts rem.

FOOT

Now knit every round until sock from start of heel shaping measures 1½in (4cm) less than required foot length. You can put the sock on and see how much further you need to go.

SHAPE TOE

Round 1
Needle 1 K to last 3 sts, k2tog, k1.
Needle 2 K1, ssk, k to last 3 sts, k2tog, k1.
Needle 3 K1, ssk, k to end of needle.

Round 2
K.

Rep last 2 rounds until a total of 28 sts rem. Then work only round 1 again until there are 20 sts left. Work across sts on needle 1, then place sts onto 2 needles and graft the toe (see page 21). Darn in any loose ends.

Fabulous furry socks

This variation is knitted to the same basic sock pattern, but this time with the addition of a tactile and glamorous fake-fur trim. As with the previous versions of the sock, the cuff is knitted straight on two needles. The work is then transferred to double-pointed needles to knit the sock itself in the round.

MATERIALS

A 2 x 1¾oz (50g) balls of light-weight (DK) wool, acrylic and nylon mix yarn in violet
B 1 x 1¾oz (50g) ball of light-weight (DK) eyelash yarn in lilac

Knit your Fabulous furry cuff...
(Make 2)

Cast on 48 sts using size 4 (3.5mm) straight needles and yarn B. Work in st st for 2in (5cm).

Evenly distribute sts onto 3 size 4 (3.5mm) dpns. Place marker to show beg of round. Break off yarn B and join in yarn A to start working in the round. Work k2, p2 rib for 1in (2.5cm).

Next round Dec 4 sts evenly in round for smallest size; inc 4 sts for largest size (no change necessary for middle size). 44 [48: 52] sts.
Cont as for Basic Sock using yarn A.

Here the decorative trim is made from a wonderfully lush eyelash yarn. The long strands of the yarn, worked here in stockinette stitch, makes up a fabric that looks and feels like feathers or fake fur.

A little extra touch

Here we show you that by taking a basic sock pattern, you can add a simple decorative feature to turn it into something special. While the two projects here may look very different, from the ankle down the pattern is worked in exactly the same way. The Celtic Cables knee-length version features extra shaping to follow the curve of your lower leg, and has a hidden ribbed band under the cabled panels that are added at the end. In the Peppermint Pompom version, the ribbed band is turned down and some playful handmade pompoms attached.

Celtic cables

 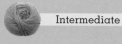

Intermediate

These socks are knitted in the round from the calf down to the toe. A ribbed section hidden under the decorative cable top and discreet shaping in the calf part of the sock means that these knee-highs will stay up tall and proud on your legs while hugging the contours snuggly. The fold-down cabled edge is worked separately and added after you've completed the main sock.

Knee-length socks will keep you wonderfully warm. The eye-catching detail on these socks is the decorative cable band around the calf. This is reminiscent of the beautiful knot patterns often seen in Celtic-inspired jewellery and designs.

Measurements

Small: calf at widest point
9½in (24cm)
Medium: calf at widest point
11in (28cm)
Large: calf at widest point
12½in (32cm)
(NB: this is the width of the sock, not of your calf – the sock will stretch to fit you snugly)

Gather together...

MATERIALS
2 x 3½oz (100g) balls of light-weight (DK) acrylic yarn in variegated blues

NEEDLES AND NOTIONS
1 set of size 4 (3.5mm) double-pointed needles
1 pair of size 5 (4mm) needles
Cable needle
Stitch marker

Gauge

19 sts and 27 rows to 4in (10cm) square measured over st st using size 4 (3.5mm) needles

tip

To make socks that fit you well, you will need to know exactly how long your feet are. You can do this by placing a piece of paper flush against a wall. Put your foot on the paper so that your heel touches the wall. Now mark where your big toe is. Measure to this point from the heel edge of the paper and you'll know how long your foot is – and how long you need to knit for!

Knit your socks...
(Make 2)

Cast on 56 [60: 64] sts using size 4 (3.5mm) double-pointed needles. Distribute sts evenly over 3 needles and join in the round, being careful not to twist the cast-on row. Place a marker to indicate the start of the round.

Work in k1, p1 rib for 1½in (4.5cm).

Now k every round for 2in (5cm), ending at the marker.

Inc round *K14 [15: 16] sts, m1, rep from * to end of round.
60 [64: 68] sts.

K every round for 2in (5cm).

Dec round *K13 [14: 15] sts, k2tog, rep from * to end of round. 56 [60: 64] sts.

K every round for 2in (5cm).

Dec round *K12 [13: 14] sts, k2tog, rep from * to end of round. 52 [56: 60] sts.

K every round for 2in (5cm).

Dec round *K11 [12: 13] sts, k2tog, rep from * to end of round. 48 [52: 56] sts.

K every round for 2in (5cm).

Dec round *K10 [11: 12] sts, k2tog, rep from * to end of round. 44 [48: 52] sts.

Cont to knit until the sock when measured against your leg reaches from just below your knee to just below your ankle bone. Everyone's calves are a different length, so you need to measure this yourself.

HEEL FLAP
Divide sts between 2 needles so that there are 22 [24: 26] sts on each needle. You will work on just one needle – the other sts will form the gusset later on. When you turn your knitting you should be ready to start on a purl row. You will work backwards and forwards in st st for the flap.

Row 1 Sl 1st st and p across row.

Next row Sl 1st st and k across row.

Rep last 2 rows 10 [11: 12] times more 22 [24: 26] rows are worked in total.

Next row Sl 1st st and p across row.

SHAPE HEEL
Sl 1, k13 [14: 15], ssk, k1, turn.
Sl 1, p7, p2tog, p1, turn.
Sl 1, k8, ssk, k1, turn.
Sl 1, p9, p2tog, p1, turn.
Sl 1, k10, ssk, k1, turn.
Cont in this way until 12 [14, 16] sts rem, ending on a purl row.

GUSSET
With spare needle, k6 [7: 8] sts from the heel needle.

Needle 1 K next 6 [7: 8] sts, then pick up and knit 12 [13: 14] sts from the side of the heel.

Needle 2 K across all 24 [26: 28] sts.

Needle 3 Pick up and knit 12 [13: 14] sts from side of heel and k across 6 [7: 8] sts on spare needle.
60 [66: 72] sts.

SHAPE GUSSET
Round 1
Needle 1 K to last 3 sts, k2tog, k1.
Needle 2 K.
Needle 3 K1, ssk, k to end of needle.

Round 2
K all three needles.

Rep last 2 rounds until:
Needle 1 11 [12: 13] sts rem.

Needle 2 22 [24: 26] sts rem.
Needle 3 11 [12: 13] sts rem.

FOOT

Now knit every round until sock from
start of heel shaping measures
1½in (4.5cm) less than required foot
length. You can try the sock on now
and see how much further you need
to go.

SHAPE TOE

Round 1
Needle 1 K to last 3 sts, k2tog, k1.
Needle 2 K1, ssk, k to last 3 sts,
k2tog, k1.
Needle 3 k1, ssk, k to end of needle.

Round 2
K all three needles.

Rep last 2 rounds until 28 sts rem
for all sizes. Then work only round
1 again until there are 20 sts left.
Work across sts on needle 1, then
place sts onto 2 needles. Then graft
the toe (see page 21).

The heel is fully shaped; the heel flap is knitted first, then the heel turned, and
stitches picked up to form the gusset. It may look tricky, but you'll feel like a genius
when you manage it, and the sock will fit you exactly.

The cabled panel is knitted separately and sewn to the top of the finished sock.
Only one size is given as it should stretch around most legs. However, before
you bind off, wrap it round your leg to see whether you need to work another
pattern repeat.

*If you are new to
working cable stitches,
you may find it easier to
use a cable needle with
a kink in it (as opposed
to a straight one), as it will help
to hold your stitches better.*

Knit your cable cuff...

Cast on 18 sts using size 5 (4mm)
needles.
Row 1 K1, p1, (k2, p2) 3 times, k2,
p1, k1.
Row 2 P1, k1, (p2, k2) 3 times, p2, k1, p1.
Rows 3, 7 and 9 As row 1.
**Row 4 and every foll even-
numbered row** As row 2.
Row 5 K1, p1, *sl 4 sts onto a cable
needle and leave at front of work,
k2, p the 2 p sts on the cable
needle, k the 2 k sts* p2, rep the

work from * to * once more, p1, k1.
Row 11 K1, p1, k2, p2, sl 4 sts on to
cable needle and leave at back
of work, k2, p the 2 p sts on cable
needle, k the 2 k sts, p2, k2, p1, k1.
Rep these 12 rows 5 more times.
Bind off.

Join the two ends using mattress
stitch (see page 21), taking care to
match up the pattern. Sew cuff onto
top of sock. Darn in any loose ends.

Peppermint pompoms

The basic pattern for these socks is an excellent starting point for crafty creativity. These ankle-length socks are knitted in the round from light-weight (DK) yarn, so there is a huge range of yarns available for you to make the socks in whatever colour and fibre you prefer. Here we've given the socks a lively twist by working them in a minty-fresh colourway and added some cute pompoms as a trim to the ribbed cuff.

Measurements

Small: foot at widest point
8¼in (21cm)

Medium: foot at widest point
9in (23cm)

Large: foot at widest point
9⁷⁄₈in (25cm)

Gather together...

MATERIALS
2 [2: 3] x 1¾oz (50g) balls of light-weight (DK) acrylic and nylon yarn in mint green

NEEDLES AND NOTIONS
1 set of size 4 (3.5mm)
    double-pointed needles
1 size E4 (3.5mm) crochet hook
Stitch marker

Gauge

19 sts and 27 rows to 4in (10cm) square measured over st st using size 4 (3.5mm) needles

Knit your socks...

(Make 2)

Cast on 44 [48: 52] sts using size 4 (3.5mm) double-pointed needles.
Distribute sts evenly over 3 needles and join to work in the round, being careful not to twist the cast-on row. Place a marker to indicate the start of the round.
Work a k1, p1 rib for 2in (5cm).
Now knit every round for 2in (5cm), ending the round at the marker.

HEEL FLAP
Divide sts between 2 needles so that there are 22 [24: 26] sts on each needle. You will work on just one needle; the other sts will form the gusset later on. When you turn your knitting you should be ready to start on a purl row. You will work backwards and forwards in st st for the flap.

Row 1 Sl 1st st and p across row.
Next row Sl 1st st and k across row.
Rep last 2 rows 10 [11: 12] times more.
    22 [24: 26] rows are worked in total.
Next row Sl 1st st and p across row.

SHAPE HEEL

Sl 1, k13 [14: 15], ssk, k1, turn.
Sl 1, p7, p2tog, p1, turn.
Sl 1, k8, ssk, k1, turn.
Sl 1, p9, p2tog, p1, turn.
Sl 1, k10, ssk, k1, turn.
Cont in this way until 12 [14: 16] sts rem, ending on a p row.

GUSSET

With spare needle k 6 [7: 8] sts from the heel needle.
Needle 1 K next 6 [7: 8] sts, then pick up and knit 12 [13: 14] sts from the side of the heel.
Needle 2 K across all 24 [26: 28] sts.

Make these cute pompoms in the same yarn as the socks. See page 23 for pompom-making instructions.

Needle 3 Pick up and knit 12 [13: 14] sts from side of heel and k across 6 [7: 8] sts on spare needle. 66 [73: 80] sts.

SHAPE GUSSET

Round 1

Needle 1 Knit to last 3 sts, k2tog, k1.

Needle 2 K.

Needle 3 K1, ssk, k to end of needle.

Round 2

Knit all three needles.

Rep last 2 rounds until:

Needle 1 11 [12: 13] sts rem.

Needle 2 22 [24: 26] sts rem.

Needle 3 11 [12: 13] sts rem.

FOOT

Now knit every round until sock from start of heel shaping measures 1½in (4.5cm) less than required foot length. You can try the sock on now and see how much further you need to go.

SHAPE TOE

Round 1

Needle 1 K to last 3 sts, k2tog, k1.

Needle 2 K1, ssk, k to last 3 sts, k2tog, k1.

Needle 3 K1, ssk, k to end of needle.

Round 2

K.

Rep the last 2 rounds until 28 sts rem for all sizes, then work round 1 only until 20 sts rem. Work across sts on needle 1, then place sts onto 2 needles and graft the toe (see page 21).

This pair of socks is knitted to the same basic pattern as the Celtic Cables, but is, of course, only ankle length. This time the embellishment comes from the addition of the funky pompoms.

Making up

Make 4 small 1½in (4.5cm) pompoms, leaving a 20in (51cm) end of the centre tying yarn. Working as close to the pompom as possible, create a slipknot and crochet a chain measuring 2½in (7cm) and fasten off. Attach 2 of the chains to the socks, as shown in the photograph.

Lingerie lace stockings

Give some love to your legs with these sumptuous stockings, made in a luscious mixture of merino wool and silk and finished with a silky ribbon to complete the lingerie look. The lacy section is made on two needles and seamed up the side, while the foot section is knitted in the round. The very top of the stocking is made in stockinette stitch. The nature of this fabric means that it will curl over itself to create the rolled-over look.

 Intermediate

Measurements

One size fits all

Gather together...

MATERIALS
5 x 1¾oz (50g) balls of light weight (DK) merino wool and silk mix yarn in purple

NEEDLES AND NOTIONS
1 pair of size 6 (4mm) needles
1 set of size 6 (4mm) double-pointed needles
Stitch holder
Stitch marker
3ft (1m) of ribbon in a co-ordinating colour

Gauge

22 sts and 30 rows to 4in (10cm) square measured over st st using size 6 (4mm) needles

Knit your stockings...

**Using size 6 (4mm) straight needles, cast on 69 sts.
Starting with a knit row, work 6 rows of st st.
Next row K6, k2tog, *k4, k2tog, rep from * to last 7 sts, k7. 59 sts.
Next row P.
Now begin the lace pattern.

LACE PATTERN
Row 1 K.
Row 2 P2tog to last st, p1.
Row 3 K1, *pick up yarn between stitches and knit, k1; rep from * to end of row.

Row 4 P1, *yo, p2tog; rep from * to end of row.

These 4 rows form lace pattern.

OVER-THE-KNEE VERSION
Rep lace patt 10 times.

BELOW-THE-KNEE VERSION
Rep lace patt 4 times.

BOTH VERSIONS
Dec 1 st at both ends of next and every following 3rd pattern repeat until 39 sts rem.

With their open, lacy pattern and ribbon flounce, these
luxurious stockings are reminiscent of those that were
worn by Hollywood starlets of the 1930s – only warmer!

OVER-THE-KNEE VERSION

Cont in lace patt until work measures
21½in (54.5cm) or length required
ending on row 4.

BELOW-THE-KNEE VERSION

Cont in lace patt for 4 more pattern
repeats.

HEEL FOR RIGHT SOCK

Next row (K1, m1) 12 times (so there
are 24 sts), leaving rem 27 sts on a
stitch holder.

Next row P.

Next row K.

Work straight in st st on these 24 sts
for 21 rows.

Next row K14, ssk, k1, turn.

Next row P6, p2tog, p1, turn.

Next row K to the stitch before the
gap, ssk, k1, turn.

Next row P to the stitch before the
gap, p2tog, p1, turn.

Rep these last 2 rows until 14 sts rem.

Change to size 6 (4mm) double-
pointed needles and beg working
in the round.

The pretty lacy pattern that gives these stockings their unique look is created
from a simple four-row pattern. It's easy to make decreases in this pattern, and the
stockings are shaped so that they follow the curve of your lower leg and fit snugly.

Next round

Needle 1 K14.

Needle 2 Pick up and knit 13 sts from
heel edge.

Needle 3 K27 from stitch holder.

Needle 4 Pick up and knit 13 sts from
heel. 67 sts.

HEEL FOR LEFT SOCK

Next row K to last 12 sts, (k1, m1) 12
times (so there are 24 sts), leaving
rem 27 sts on a stitch holder.

Next row P.

Next row K.

Work straight in st st on these 24 sts
for 21 rows.

Next row K14, ssk, k1, turn.

Next row P6, p2tog, p1, turn.

Next row K to stitch before the gap,
ssk, k1, turn.

Next row P to stitch before the gap,
p2tog, p1, turn.

Rep these last 2 rows until 14 sts rem.

Change to size 6 (4mm) double-
pointed needles and beg working
in the round.

Next round

Needle 1 K14.

Needle 2 Pick up and knit 13 sts from
heel edge.

Needle 3 K27 from stitch holder.

Needle 4 Pick up and knit 13 sts from
heel. 67 sts.

BOTH SOCKS

Round 1

Needle 1 K7, place stitch marker, k7.

Needle 2 K to last 3 sts, k2tog, k1.

Needle 3 K2tog to last st, k1.

Needle 4 K1, ssk, knit to end of
needle.

Round 2

Needle 1 K.

Needle 2 K.

Needle 3 K1, *pick up yarn between
sts and knit, k1; rep from * to end of
needle.

Needle 4 K.

Round 3

Needle 1 K.

Needle 2 As needle 2, round 1.

Needle 3 K1, *yo, k2tog; rep from *to
end of needle.

Needle 4 As needle 4 of round 1.

Round 4

K all sts.

tip

_In Row 3 of the lace
pattern, you need to pick
up yarn between the
stitches to make the next
stitch. This is a fairly
simple technique: there should
be quite a clear horizontal strand
lying at the back of the work
between the stitches. Pick it up
with the tip of your left-hand
needle and loop it on to your
right-hand needle. Then knit this
strand as a normal knit stitch._

The below-the-knee version is worked in a sumptuously soft dove-grey alpaca yarn, and finished off with a dark purple ribbon.

Rep these last 4 rounds until 45 sts rem.

Next round K all sts, knitting the 1st and last sts tog at end of round. 44 sts.

Keeping patt correct, but with no further shaping, cont on these sts until foot measures 7in (19cm) or desired length, ending on round 4.

BOTH TOES

Next round (starting from stitch marker) K8, k2tog, k2, ssk, k16, k2tog, k2, ssk, k8.

Next round K.

Next round K7, k2tog, k2, ssk, k14, k2tog, k2, ssk, k7.

Next round K.

Next round K6, k2tog, k2, ssk, k12, k2tog, k2, ssk, k6.

Cont in this way until 20 sts rem.

Next round K2, k2tog, k2, ssk, k4, k2tog, k2, ssk, k2. 16 sts.

Next round K1, k2tog, k2, ssk, k2, k2tog, k2, ssk, k2. 12 sts.

Next round K2tog, k2, ssk, k2tog, k2, ssk. 8 sts.

Bind off using the 3-needle method (see page 20).

Making up

Darn in all the loose ends. Sew up the side of the sock. Weave in ribbon.

Luxury knee-highs

MATERIALS

4 x 1¾oz (50g) balls of light-weight (DK) alpaca yarn in blue-grey

Riding the wave socks

Cashmere is the queen of yarns, and your feet will think they've gone to sock heaven when you wear this sumptuously soft pair. These socks are worked in the round in a vibrant turquoise yarn. The contrasting trim of aqua and turquoise is worked in rippling crochet stitches around the cuff to form a wave pattern. If you've never crocheted before, here's your chance to see what it has to offer! Crochet techniques are explained on pages 24–25.

    Intermediate

Measurements

One size fits all

Gather together...

MATERIALS
A 3 x $^7/_8$oz (25g) skeins medium-weight (aran) pure cashmere yarn in turquoise
B 1 x $^7/_8$oz (25g) skein medium-weight (aran) pure cashmere yarn in aqua

NEEDLES AND NOTIONS
1 set of size 7 (4.5mm) double-pointed needles
1 size 7 (4.50mm) crochet hook
Stitch marker

Gauge

17 sts and 23 rows to 4in (10cm) square measured over st st using size 7 (4.5mm) needles

Special note

The crochet instructions are given in US terms. See page 24 to translate into UK terms.

Knit your socks...

(Make 2)

Cast on 40 sts using size 7 (4.5mm) double-pointed needles and yarn A.
Divide sts onto three needles, placing marker to show beg of round.
Knit for 14 rounds.

HEEL FLAP
K first 18 sts onto needle 1, leaving rem 22 sts on needles 2 and 3.
Work only sts on needle 1 as follows:

Row 1 Sl 1st st purlwise, p to end of needle, turn.

Row 2 Sl 1st st knitwise, k to end of needle.
Rep last 2 rows 8 more times.

SHAPE HEEL
Row 19 Sl 1st st purlwise, p to end.
Row 20 Sl 1st st, k9, ssk, k1.
Row 21 Sl 1st st, p3, p2tog, p1.
Row 22 Sl 1st st, k4 ssk, k1.
Row 23 Sl 1st st, p5, p2tog, p1.
Row 24 Sl 1st st, k6, ssk, k1.
Row 25 Sl 1st st, p7, p2tog, p1.
Row 26 Sl 1st st, k8, ssk.
Row 27 Sl 1st st, p8, p2tog. 10 sts left on needle.

Cashmere is the champagne of yarns, both in quality and price. A small project like these socks is ideal if you want a taste of luxury but can only afford a few skeins. You'll certainly feel like a pampered princess when you wear them! This version uses beautiful ocean-blue yarns, and the wavy crochet trim around the cuff rolls like the surf on the sea.

The crocheted trim is added once the main section of the sock has been knitted. Make a round of slip stitches around the top of the cuff to create a foundation row for the crochet, then work the wave pattern. Ripple stitches in stripes of contrasting colours add a pleasing detail.

GUSSET

Place rem 22 sts onto one needle.

Knit across 5 heel sts with spare needle.

Needle 1 Knit across next 5 sts with another needle, placing marker after 1st st. Pick up and knit 12 sts from side of the heel.

Needle 2 Work across the 22 sts.

Needle 3 Pick up and knit 12 sts from the other side of the heel and knit across the final 5 sts. 56 sts.

SHAPE GUSSET

Round 1

Needle 1 Knit to last 3 sts, k2tog, k1.

Needle 2 K.

Needle 3 K1, ssk, k to end of needle.

Round 2

Knit all 3 needles.

Rep last 2 rounds until:

Needle 1 10 sts rem.

Needle 2 22 sts.

Needle 3 10 sts rem.

FOOT

Now knit every round until sock measures 1½in (4cm) less than required foot length. You can try the sock on now and see how much further you need to go.

SHAPE TOE

Round 1

Needle 1 K to last 3 sts, k2tog, k1.

Needle 2 K1, ssk, k to last 3 sts, k2tog, ssk.

Needle 3 k1, ssk, k to end of needle.

Round 2

Knit all three needles.

Rep last 2 rounds until a total of 20 sts rem. Then work round 1 again until 12 sts rem. Place sts onto 2 needles, then graft the toe (see page 21).

CROCHET CUFF

Using yarn B and a size 7 (4.50mm) crochet hook, work a round of 39 sl sts around top of sock.

**Next round Chain 3, 2 dc, 3 dc into next st, 3 dc, *miss next st, 3 dc, 3 dc into next st, 3 dc, rep from * to end of round.

Rep from ** using yarn B, then work 2 rounds in yarn A, then 1 round in yarn B, then 1 round in yarn A. Fasten off.

Darn in any loose ends.

Monochrome magic

MATERIALS

A 2 x 1¾oz (50g) balls of medium-weight (aran) cashmere and merino wool blend yarn in black

B 1 x 1¾oz (50g) ball of medium-weight (aran) cashmere and merino wool blend yarn in off-white

tip

When working with cashmere you may want to cover your lap with a towel or piece of material as cashmere yarn has a tendency to shed its fibres.

Update your wardrobe with these fabulous monochrome socks. The classic black and white colour scheme still dominates the fashion pages, so why not knit yourself some socks to match?

Short and sweet sockettes

These cute socks are deliberately made with a very short cuff; they're meant to be shown off with trainers or tennis shoes, so only the quirkily embellished cuffs are visible above shoes. These sockettes are knitted in the round, with a fully shaped heel. The cuff (which is covered up by the decorations) is ribbed for a good fit. This is another great example of how you can give a project your own individual twist; we've given you some ideas for decorations, but exercise your ingenuity and come up with some more!

 Simple

Measurements

One size fits all

Gather together...

MATERIALS
2 x 1¾oz (50g) balls of light-weight (DK) extra-fine merino wool and angora mix yarn in cream
or 2 x 1¾oz (50g) balls of light-weight (DK) alpaca and silk mix yarn in lilac

NEEDLES AND NOTIONS
1 set of size 6 (4mm) double-pointed needles
Pompoms or buttons for decorating the cuff
Stitch marker

Gauge

22 sts and 28 rows to 4in (10cm) square measured over st st using size 6 (4mm) needles

Knit your socks...
(Make 2)

Using size 6 (4mm) double-pointed needles, cast on 48 sts and divide evenly among 3 needles.
Add a stitch marker at the beginning of the round to mark the start of the round.
Round 1 (K1, p1) for whole round.
Cont in 1x1 rib as set until work measures 1in (2.5cm).
Knit 3 rounds.

HEEL FLAP
Next row K 12 sts, turn.
Next row P 24 sts.
Work straight on these 24 sts for 22 rows.

SHAPE HEEL
Next row K14 sts, ssk, k1, turn.
Next row P6, p2tog, p1, turn.
Next row K to the stitch before the gap, ssk, k1, turn.
Next row P to the stitch before the gap, p2tog, p1, turn.

These sockettes are made to a simple pattern – the real fun comes in choosing the embellishments for the cuff! They're meant to be seen, so make them as bold and bright as you like.

Rep these last 2 rows until 14 sts rem, ending on a p row.

Next row K.

GUSSET

Next round Pick up and knit 13 sts from side of heel, placing stitch marker after last st.

Knit 24 sts from the next needle.

With the 3rd needle, pick up and knit 13 sts (placing a stitch marker before the 1st st) from side of the heel and knit 7 sts from the 1st needle. 64 sts.

SHAPE GUSSET

Next round K to the 3 sts before 1st stitch marker, k2tog, k1, k to next stitch marker, k1, ssk, k to end of round. 62 sts.

Next round K.

Rep these last 2 rounds until 44 sts.

FOOT

Cont on these sts until foot measures 6in (15.5cm) or desired length for the foot.

SHAPE TOE

Round 1 Knit to 3 sts before 1st stitch marker, k2tog, k1, slip marker, k1, ssk, knit to 3 sts before 2nd stitch marker, k2tog, k1, slip marker, k1, ssk, k to end. 40 sts.

Round 2 K.

Cont to dec in this way, either side of each stitch marker, until 20 sts rem. Then repeat round 1 until 8 sts rem.

Bind off using the 3-needle method (see page 20).

Making up

Darn in any loose ends. With a matching sewing cotton, sew on the pompoms or buttons over the rib cuff.

When adding your embellishments, stitch a few on at a time, then secure the thread. If any come off, you will only lose one or two.

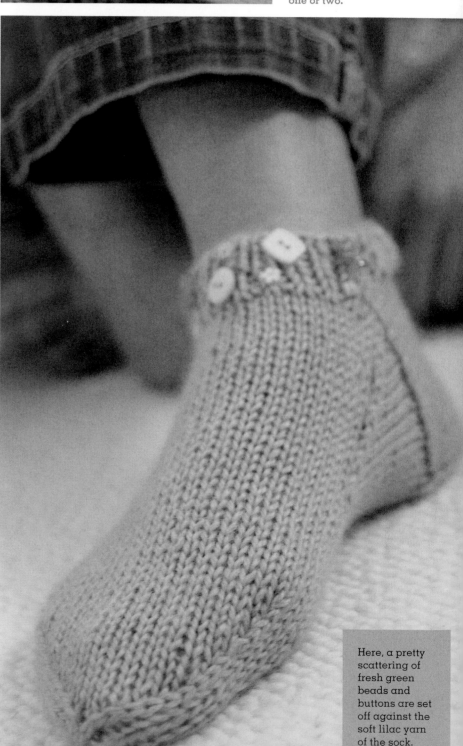

Here, a pretty scattering of fresh green beads and buttons are set off against the soft lilac yarn of the sock.

Embellish

Be imaginative with your choice of trimmings for the cuff. You could use fabric shapes, ribbon flowers, and tiny seed beads as decorations. In fact, you can use nearly any sort of trimming as long as it can be hand-washed, so most things will work. However, note that iron-on patches won't work as they have no stretch in them, and all the embellishments should be stitched into place.

Soothing the sole...

Ballerina bliss slippers

Get in touch with your inner diva and take a twirl in these gorgeous slippers. Modelled on the classic, elegant shape of ballet shoes, they're perfect for blissing out in your boudoir, or just hanging out at home. Make the slippers in vibrant colours and experiment with embellishments – beads, buttons, sequins and embroidery. There are many ways to make your ballet shoes beautiful.

Simple

Measurements

Small [Medium: Large]

Gather together...

MATERIALS
1 x 3½oz (100g) ball of light-weight (DK) acrylic yarn in bright pink

NEEDLES AND NOTIONS
1 pair of size 6 (4mm) needles
1 size G6 (4.00mm) crochet hook
Artificial flower petals
Contrasting bead for centre of flower

Gauge

22 sts and 30 rows to 4in (10cm) square measured over st st using size 6 (4mm) needles

Special note

The crochet instructions are given in US terms. See page 24 to translate into UK terms.

Knit your slippers...
(Make 2)

SOLE
Cast on 12 [12: 14] sts using size 6 (4mm) needles.
Row 1 K.
Row 2 P1, pfb, k8 [8: 10], pfb, p1. 14 [14: 16] sts.
Row 3 K.
Row 4 P1, pfb, k10 [10: 12], pfb, p1. 16 [16: 18] sts.
Row 5 K.
Row 6 P1, pfb, k12 [12: 14], pfb, p1. 18 [18: 20] sts.**
Work 53 [55: 57] rows in st st.
Next row P1, p2tog, k10 [12: 14], p2tog tbl, p1. 16 [16: 18] sts.
Next row K.
Next row P1, p2tog, k8 [10: 12], p2tog tbl, p1. 14 [14: 16] sts.

These slippers are knitted flat on straight needles and then the two sides of the heel are seamed together.

Next row K.
Next row P1, p2tog, k6 [8: 10], p2tog tbl, p1. 12 [12: 14] sts.
Next row K.
Bind off.

These lovely slippers are made
in simple stockinette stitch in
a hard-wearing acrylic yarn.
You can dress them up however
you like; here, we embellished
the slippers with a vivid yellow
artificial flower that contrasts
boldly with the hot pink.

TOP OF SLIPPER

Work as for sole to **.

Work 18 rows in st st.

Next row K8 [8: 9] sts, bind off 2 sts, k8 [8: 9] sts. 16 [16: 18] sts.

Next row Working on first 8 [8: 9] sts only, p.

Next row K2tog tbl, k to end. 7 [7: 8] sts.

Next row P.

Next row K2tog tbl, k to end. 6 [6: 7] sts.

Next row P.

Work 10 [10: 12] rows in st st ending on P row.

Next row K1, m1, k5 [5: 6] sts. 7 [7: 8] sts.

Work 7 rows in st st.

Next row K1, m1, k6 [6: 7] sts. 8 [8: 9] sts.

Work 9 rows in st st.

Next row K1, m1, k7 [7: 8] sts. [9 [9: 10] sts.

Next row P.

Bind off.

Rejoin yarn to rem sts and rep for other side, reversing shapings.

The slippers are finished off with a crocheted trim around the opening.

Making up

With right sides facing, join sole to top of foot.

CROCHET EDGING

With size G6 (4.00mm) crochet hook, work a round of single crochet in a number divisible by 4.

Next round Chain 1, work 2 sc into next 2 sts, *miss 1 st, work 3 sc, rep from * to end. Fasten off.

More dancing divas

MATERIALS

Embroidered version: 1 x 3½oz (100g) ball of light-weight (DK) acrylic yarn in yellow

Buttons version: 1 x 3½oz (100g) ball of light-weight (DK) acrylic yarn in turquoise

Beaded version: 1 x 3½oz (100g) ball of light-weight (DK) acrylic yarn in purple

Add the petals of an artificial flower to the slipper and secure in place with a contrasting bead.

STRAPPING STYLE

Make some straps to help keep the slippers stay on your feet.

Knit the strap:

Cast on 3 sts.

Work in garter st (every row knit) until strap measures 5in (12.5cm).

Bind off.

Using the photograph as a guide, attach one side of the strap(s) to the inside of the slipper where the crochet edge meets the knitting edge. Attach the other end to the outside of the slipper on the other side. Finish by sewing a button onto the end of the strap.

Inspiration

Here is some inspiration for how you can embellish your slippers:

• Using a contrasting yarn, embroider a spiral pattern.
• Add some matching buttons in a random pattern using a strong thread.
• Using strong sewing thread, attach beads in the shape of a snowflake.

Adding straps also gives a different look, and the variations are endless. See opposite page for instructions on adding them.

Snowflake specials

The slippers and socks featured in this section are knitted using medium-weight (aran) pure wool yarn. This is a rather heavy yarn to use for socks, but it makes a tough, dense fabric. Whether you are relaxing around the house, or walking in the countryside in galoshes or wellies, the socks will keep your feet toasty warm in the most wintry of weather. The designs are Scandinavian in feel, with the additional sparkle of the embroidered snowflakes and the vividly contrasting scarlet and cream colourways.

Swedish felted slippers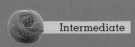

Intermediate

These slippers have been fulled to make the fabric even denser. The process of fulling shrinks the fabric and loses the definition of the individual stitches, so it looks like felt (hence the process can also be known as felting). The sole of the slipper, the top, and the sides are all made separately by knitting straight on two needles and the pieces then stitched together. The stitches for the cuff are picked up from the top and then worked in the round.

These fabulous felted slippers are based on a Swedish style; the blanket stitch and snowflake designs are common in Swedish folk fashions. The slippers are knitted larger than the given shoe size and then fulled to shrink them to the correct proportions. The fulling process makes the slippers tough enough to be worn as indoor footwear.

Measurements

Small [Medium: Large]

Gather together...

MATERIALS

5 x 1¾oz (50g) balls of medium-weight (aran) wool and alpaca mix yarn in red

Oddment of light-weight (DK) wool yarn in cream for embroidery

NEEDLES AND NOTIONS

1 pair of size 9 (5.5mm) needles
1 set of size 7 (4.5mm) double-pointed needles
Embroidery needle

Gauge

Before fulling: 16.5 sts and 22 rows to 4in (10cm) square measured over st st using size 9 (5.5mm) needles

Special note

The slippers are knitted larger than these proportions and then fulled to shrink down to the given size.

Use this photograph as a guide for adding the embroidered snowflakes. These details are made in cream light-weight (DK) yarn to make a vivid contrast against the warm red yarn used for the slipper.

Knit your slippers...

(Make 2)

SOLE OF SLIPPER

Cast on 16 sts.
Row 1 K1, kfb, k12, kfb, k1. 18 sts.
Row 2 P.
Row 3 K1, kfb, k14, kfb, k1. 20 sts.
Row 4 P.
Row 5 K1, kfb, k16, kfb, k1. 22 sts.
Row 6 P. *
Work 38 [40: 42] rows in st st.
Next row K1, k2tog, k16, k2tog tbl, k1. 20 sts.
Next row P.
Next row K1, k2tog, k14, k2tog tbl, k1. 18 sts.
Next row P.
Next row K1, k2tog, k12, k2tog tbl, k1. 16 sts.
Next row P.
Bind off.

TOP OF SLIPPER

Work as for sole to *.
Work 30 [33: 34] rows in st st.
Next row K6, bind off 10 sts, k6.
Now work on only the 1st 6 sts.
Next row P.
Next row K1, k2tog tbl, k3. 5 sts.

Next row P.
Next row K.
Next row P.
Next row K1, kfb, k3. 6 sts.
Next row P.

With WS facing, rejoin yarn to rem 6 sts and work on just these.
Next row P.
Next row K3, k2tog, k1. 5 sts.
Next row P.
Next row K.
Next row P.
Next row K3, kfb, k1. 6 sts.

Cast on 10 sts, turn and k across the first 6 sts. 22 sts.
Next row P all sts.
Next row K1, k2tog tbl, k across all sts to last 3 sts, k2tog, k1. 20 sts.
Next row P.
Next row K1, k2tog tbl, k across all sts to last 3 sts, k2tog, k1. 18 sts.
Next row P.
Next row K1, k2tog tbl, k across all sts to last 3 sts, k2tog, k1. 16 sts.
Next row P.
Bind off.

SIDE OF SLIPPER

Cast on 7 sts.
Work in st st for 10 [10¼: 10½]in (26.5 [27: 27.5]cm).
Bind off.

CUFF OF SLIPPER

With right side facing, pick up and knit 40 sts using size 7 (4.5mm) double-pointed needles around opening in the top of slipper.

Working in the round, k every row until cuff measures 7in (18cm).

Making up

Darn in any loose ends.

With wrong sides facing, join both ends of the side section.

Now join the side to the sole of foot using back stitch on the right side so that a ridge is made.

Repeat this for the top of the slipper.

Fold the cuff over with the purl side showing and attach the bound-off edge to the pick-up sts point.

FULLING

Place slippers in washing machine and wash on a 40-degree cycle. Let the slippers dry naturally.

FINISHING

Using the photograph as a guide, embroider snowflake designs to the top of the slipper and work blanket stitch around the top ridge.

To make the cuff, stitches are picked up from the opening in the top of the slipper. The cuff is then knitted in the round in stockinette stitch, and folded down so the purl side shows on the outside. The cuff is then stitched into place around the base.

tip

When the slippers are drying, stuff the inside with scrunched-up newspaper so that they keep their shape well.

A trim of blanket stitch (see page 22) in cream yarn is added to the top ridge of the slipper. This creates a pleasing embellishment and emphasizes the ridge, which is creating by back-stitching the slipper side to the top of the slipper. All the embroidery is added after the slippers have been fulled.

Fulling

The success of this design lies in fulling the slippers after they have been knitted and made up. The fulling process 'shrinks' the knitted fabric, and makes it denser, tougher and warmer, so it resembles felt.

Felting occurs when the knitted fabric is placed in hot water with soap and agitated. This process makes the yarn fibres shrink and mesh together. Note that not all yarns will felt – cotton and synthetic fibres, for example, don't felt at all. You need to use a yarn that is either 100 per cent wool, or one that contains a high percentage of wool blended with other yarn or yarns that will also felt.

You can full knitted items by hand, alternating between hot and cold water, but the easiest and quickest method is to use a washing machine. Use laundry soap or soap flakes rather than ordinary washing powder or detergent, and set the machine to a higher temperature than recommended for washing woollens (40 degrees should be sufficient).

The degree of shrinkage obtained from fulling can be unpredictable, so it's best to do a swatch test first.

unfelted

felted

Winter wonderland socks

 Simple

These super-cosy winter-weather socks are knitted using needles smaller than those recommended on the ball band to make the fabric a little stiffer and denser, and therefore warmer. These socks are knitted in the round with a fully shaped heel. A hidden rib underneath the fold-down cuff will ensure that the sock fits you snugly. The design is embellished with contrast-colour snowflake designs.

Measurements

One size fits all

Gather together...

MATERIALS

3 x 1¾oz (50g) balls of medium-weight (aran) wool and alpaca mix yarn in red

Oddment of light-weight (DK) wool yarn in cream for embroidery

NEEDLES AND NOTIONS

1 set of size 7 (4.5mm) double-pointed needles
Stitch marker
Embroidery needle

Gauge

18 sts and 26 rows to 4in (10cm) square measured over st st using size 7 (4.5mm) needles

Knit your socks...

(Make 2)

Cast on 35 sts using size 7 (4.5mm) double-pointed needles and divide equally over 3 needles, placing marker to show the start of round.
Purl for 8 rounds.
Next round Inc in 1st st at beg of round. 36 sts.
Work k1, p1 rib for 8 rounds.
Next round K.
Rep last round for 13 more rows.

HEEL FLAP

Knit 1st 18 sts onto needle 1, leaving rem 18 sts on needles 2 and 3.
Working only sts on needle 1:
Row 1 Sl 1st st purlwise, p to end of needle, turn.
Row 2 Sl 1st st knitwise, k to end of needle.
Rep last 2 rows 7 more times.

SHAPE HEEL

Row 17 Sl 1, p to end.
Row 18 Sl 1, k10, ssk, k1.
Row 19 Sl 1, p5, p2tog, p1.
Row 20 Sl 1, k6 ssk, k1.
Row 21 Sl 1, p7, p2tog, p1.
Cont in this way until 12 sts rem.

Now place other 18 sts onto 1 needle.

The top of the sock and the cuff are livened up by the addition of snowflakes embroidered in a contrasting cream yarn.

GUSSET

Knit across 6 heel sts with 1 needle.
Needle 1 Knit across next 6 sts with another needle. Then pick up and knit 11 sts from side of heel.
Needle 2 Work across the 18 sts.
Needle 3 Pick up and knit 11 sts from the other side of the heel and knit across the final 6 sts. 58 sts.

SHAPE GUSSET

Round 1
Needle 1 Knit to last 3 sts, k2tog, k1.
Needle 2 K.
Needle 3 K1, ssk, k to end of needle.

Round 2
Knit all 3 needles.

Rep last 2 rounds until:
Needle 1 9 sts rem.
Needle 2 18 sts.
Needle 3 9 sts rem.

FOOT

Now knit every round until sock
measures 1½in (4.5cm) less than
required foot length. You can try
the sock on now and see how much
further you need to go.

SHAPE TOE

Round 1
Needle 1 K to last 3 sts, k2tog, k1.
Needle 2 K1, ssk, k to last 3 sts,
    k2tog, k1.
Needle 3 K1, ssk, k to end of needle.

Round 2
K.

Rep last 2 rounds until 20 sts rem.
    Then work only round 1 again
    until 12 sts rem. Work across sts
    on needle 1, then place sts onto 2
    needles and graft toe (see page 21)

Making up

Darn in any loose ends.
Fold the top of the sock over so that
it covers the rib section, and sew in
place along the cast-on edge.
Using the photograph as a guide,
embroider snowflakes onto the sock
using cream yarn.

tip

*To measure how long
to knit the foot before
shaping the toe, turn
the sock the right way
out on your needles and
put it on your foot.*

These sturdy
socks are knitted
in the round
from the top
down. The cuff is
knitted in reverse
stockinette stitch,
so that when the
cuff is folded
down and stitched
into place, the knit
side of the fabric
shows on the
outside. A ribbed
section that is
hidden under the
cuff improves the
fit of the sock.

Gorilla feet slippers

Introduce some animal magic into your knitting with these super-fun, super-furry gorilla feet slippers for the man in your life. We made them in silvery-grey and black for a silverback option, but you could make them in brown or plain black – or, if you want to go really over the top, knit them in an exuberant colour like orange or bright blue. Both the soles and the tops of the slippers are knitted straight on two needles. The top of the slipper is made to be larger than the sole; this allows for the girth of the foot and makes the foot more furry.

  Intermediate

Measurements

Men's sizes:
Small [Medium: Large]

Gather together...

MATERIALS
A 1 x 1¾oz (50g) ball of medium-weight (aran) merino wool, microfibre and cashmere mix yarn in black
B 3 x 1¾oz (50g) balls of fake-fur eyelash yarn in black and silvery-grey

NEEDLES AND NOTIONS
1 pair of size 9 (5.5mm) needles

Gauge

Using yarn A: 19 sts and 24 rows to 4in (10cm) square measured over st st using size 9 (5.5mm) needles

Knit your feet...

RIGHT SOLE
(Note: this is worked in rev st st from the heel, so the purl side will be the right side.)

Cast on 14 [14: 16] sts using size 9 (5.5mm) needles and yarn A.
Work in rev st st starting with a purl row, increasing 1 st at both ends of row when knitting measures 1½in (4cm), 3in (8cm), 4¾in (12cm) and 7in (18cm). 22 [22: 24] sts.
Cont in rev st st until sole measures 8¼in (21cm) [8½in/22.5cm: 9¼in/24.5cm] ending with wrong side facing.

Shape big toe
Next row K1, m1, k7, turn. (You'll work on just these sts to form toe.)
Next row P.
Next row K1, m1, k8.
Cont in rev st st until toe measures 1½in (4cm) ending with WS facing.
Next row K2tog, k6, k2tog.
Next row P.
Next row Bind off after working the first 2 sts tog.

The sole and the top of the slippers are knitted separately; the sole is made in plain black medium-weight (aran) yarn, and the top in an exuberant eyelash yarn.

Shape toe section

Rejoin yarn to rem sts and work in rev st st until toe section measures 1½in (4cm), ending with WS facing.

Next row K to last 2 sts, k2tog.

Next row P.

Next row Bind off but knit the last 2 sts of the row tog.

LEFT SOLE

(Note: this is worked in rev st st from the heel, so the purl side will be the right side.)

Cast on 14 [14: 16] sts using size 9 (5.5mm) needles and yarn A.

Work in rev st st starting with a purl row, increasing 1 st at both ends of row when knitting measures 1½in (4cm), 3in (8cm), 4¾in (12cm) and 7in (18cm). 22 [22: 24] sts.

Cont in rev st st until sole measures 8¼in (21cm) [8½in/22.5cm: 9¼in/ 24.5cm] ending with wrong side facing.

Shape toe section

Next row K14 [14: 16], turn.

Work in rev st st until toe section measures 1½in (4cm) ending with WS facing.

Next row K2tog, k to end.

Next row P.

Next row Bind off after working first 2 sts tog.

Shape big toe

Rejoin yarn to rem sts and k7, m1, k1.

Next row P.

Next row K8, m1, k1.

Cont in rev st st until toe measures 1½in (4cm) ending with WS facing.

Next row K2tog, k6, k2tog.

Next row P.

Next row Bind off but knit the last 2 sts of the row together.

One fun feature of these furry slippers is the individually shaped section for the big toe – for that authentic pawprint look!

TOP OF RIGHT FOOT

(Worked from toe end.)

Big toe

Cast on 8 sts using size 9 (5.5mm) needles and yarn B.

Next row P.

Next row K7, kfb in last st. 9 sts.

Next row P.

Next row K8, kfb in last st. 10 sts.

Next row P.

Next row K9, kfb in last st. 11 sts.

Cont in rev st st until toe measures 2in (5cm) ending with a wrong side row facing. Leave sts on needle and break yarn.

Rest of toe section

Cast on 19 [20: 22] sts using size 9 (5.5mm) needles and yarn B.

Work 2in (5cm) rev st st ending with a wrong side row facing.

Rest of foot

Now knit across both sections of knitting so that they become joined.

Cont in rev st st until work measures 6½in (17cm) [7in/18cm: 7½in/19cm] from cast-on edge of toe section.

Next row K15 [15: 16] sts, bind off 0 [1: 1] st, k to end of row.

Now working on the first 15 [15: 16] sts, cont in rev st st until foot measures 11¼in (29cm) [11¾in/30cm: 12in/31cm] from cast-on edge, then bind off.

Rejoin yarn and repeat with the rem sts.

TOP OF LEFT FOOT

(Worked from toe end.)

Rest of toe section

Cast on 19 [20: 22] sts using size 9 (5.5mm) needles and yarn B.

Work 2in (5cm) rev st st ending with

WS row facing. Leave sts on needle and break yarn.

Big toe

Cast on 8 sts using size 9 (5.5mm) needles and yarn B.

Next row P.

Next row Kfb in 1st st, k7. 9 sts.

Next row P.

Next row Kfb in 1st st, k8. 10 sts.

Next row P.

Next row Kfb in 1st st, k9. 11 sts.

Cont in rev st st until toe measures 2in (5cm) ending with WS row facing.

Now knit across both sections of knitting so that they become joined.

Cont in rev st st until work measures 6½in (17cm) [7in/18cm: 7½in/19cm] from cast-on edge of toe section.

Next row K15 [15: 16] sts, bind off 0 [1: 1] st, k to end of row.

Now working on the first 15 [15: 16] sts, cont in rev st st until foot measures 11¼in (29cm) [11¾in/ 30cm: 12in/31cm] from cast-on edge, then bind off.

Rejoin yarn and repeat with the rem sts.

Making up

Darn in any loose ends. Join the two bound-off edges of the top of foot. With wrong sides facing, sew sole section to the top of the foot; the joined bound-off edges will form the back of the slipper. Because the top of the foot is larger than the sole, you will need to pin it in place first to ensure that it doesn't move.

Turn the slipper right-side out, and with the tip of your needle, gently tease the pile of the furry yarn through to the right side.

tip *To make your slippers look more realistically furry, use a comb to smooth the fibres out and make them all fall in the same direction.*

Sleeping partners

When cold weather makes you want to stay wrapped up in your duvet all day, or whenever you feel like some extra cosseting, these cosy bedsocks and hot-water bottle cover are just what you need. They are made from a luscious blend of merino wool and angora yarn, combining warmth with sumptuous strokability. The pretty lilac shade is just the colour therapy required to help you relax and drift off into a heavenly night's sleep.

Intermediate

Curly cuff bedsocks

These lovely lilac-coloured socks are knitted straight on two needles and seamed up the back. The cuff features a twisted rib pattern, while the main body of the sock is made in stockinette stitch. Make the matching hot-water bottle cover (pages 77–79), and you're ready for bed!

Measurements

Small [Medium: Large]

Gather together...

MATERIALS
2 x 1¾oz (50g) balls of extra-fine merino wool and angora blend yarn in lilac

NEEDLES AND NOTIONS
1 pair of size 6 (4mm) needles

Gauge

22 sts and 28 rows to 4in (10cm) measured over st st using size 6 (4mm) needles

Snuggle up and have the sweetest of dreams with these super-soft bedsocks and hot-water bottle cover. They're made in a pretty-coloured yarn in textured stitches that make these items even more robust and cosy.

Knit your socks...

(Make 2)

Using size 6 (4mm) needles, cast on 56 sts.

Row 1 (RS) P2, *yon, k1, yon, p2; rep from * to end of row.

Row 2 K2, *p3, k2; rep from * to end of row.

Row 3 P2, *k3, p2; rep from * to end of row.

Row 4 K2, *p3tog, k2; rep from * to end of row.

These 4 rows form the twisted rib pattern.

Repeat these 4 rows 8 times (32 rows in all).

Then, starting with a knit row, work 6 rows in st st.

SHAPE HEEL

Next row K15 sts, turn.

Next row Starting with a knit row, work 14 rows in st st.

Next row K1, k2tog, k1, turn.

Next row P.

Next row K2, k2tog, k1, turn.

Next row P.

Next row K3, k2tog, K1, turn.

Next row P.

Next row K4, k2tog, k1, turn.

Next row P.

Next row K5, k2tog K1, turn.

Next row P.

Next row K6, k2tog, k1, turn.

Next row P.

Next row K7, k2tog, pick up 8 sts along the heel side. Knit the rest of the stitches. 57 sts.

Next row P15 sts.

Next row Work 14 rows in st st.

Next row P1, p2tog, p1, turn.

Next row K.

Next row P2, p2tog, p1, turn.

Next row K.

Next row P3, p2tog, p1, turn.

Next row K.

Next row P4, p2tog, p1, turn.

Next row K.

Next row P5, p2tog, p1, turn.

Next row K.

Next row P6, p2tog, p1, turn.

Next row K.

Next row P7, p2tog, pick up 8 sts. Purl the rest of the stitches. 58 sts.

Next row K.

Next row P.

Next row K14, k2tog, k28, ssk, k14.

Next row P.

Next row K13, k2tog, k28, ssk, k13.

Next row P.

Next row K12, k2tog, k28, ssk, k12.

Next row P.

Next row K11, k2tog, k28, ssk, k11.

Next row P.

Next row K10, k2tog, k28, ssk, k10.

Next row P.

Next row K9, k2tog, k28, ssk, k9.

Next row P.

Next row K8, k2tog, k28, ssk, k8. 46 sts.

Cont working on these 46 sts until work measures 5 [6: 7]in (12.5: 15: 17.75cm) from the back of the heel.

SHAPE TOE

Next row K9, k2tog, k1, ssk, k18, k2tog, k1, ssk, k9. 42 sts.

Next row P.

Next row K8, k2tog, k1, ssk, k16, k2tog, k1, ssk, k8. 38 sts.

Next row P.

Cont decreasing in this way until 26 sts rem.

Next row K5, k2tog, k1, ssk, k10, k2tog, k1, ssk, k5. 22 sts.

Next row K4, k2tog, k1, ssk, k8, k2tog, k1, ssk, k4. 18 sts.

Cont decreasing in this way until 6 sts rem.

Bind off.

Making up

Darn in any loose ends. Sew up the back and toe seams.

The twisted rib pattern on the sock cuffs makes for an eye-catching detail. This is a simple stitch created with four-row repeats.

tip *These socks are knitted on two needles, with a seam running from the cuff to the toe under your foot. Use mattress stitch (see page 21) to join the seams; this gives you a nice flat seam that will be comfortable on your foot.*

Seed stitch softie

This hot-water bottle cover is sublimely soft, and made in a double seed stitch pattern that gives it extra depth and texture. The pocket in the front lets you tuck in some dried lavender; the warmth from the hot-water bottle will release the aroma and help soothe you to sleep. The cover has buttons at the back so you can easily remove the hot-water bottle to empty and refill it. The buttonholes are made using a cable cast-on (see page 12).

Measurements

8in wide by 10in long
(20 x 25.5cm)

Gather together...

MATERIALS
4 x 1¾oz (50g) balls of extra-fine merino wool and angora mix yarn in lilac

NEEDLES AND NOTIONS
1 pair of size 9 (5.5mm) needles
Stitch holder
4 pearl buttons
Standard-size hot-water bottle
Popper fastener

Gauge

20 sts and 24 rows to 4in (10cm) square measured over double seed stitch (UK: double moss stitch) using size 9 (5.5mm) needles and the yarn doubled.

Knit note

The yarn is used double throughout this pattern; make sure you knit through both strands of yarn for each stitch.

Special note

Double seed stitch (UK: double moss stitch) pattern:
Row 1 (k1, p1) to end of row.
Rows 2 and 4 Knit the k sts and purl the p sts.
Row 3 (p1, k1) to end of row.

tip
Use long pins when pinning the knitting together. These will help to hold the pieces firmly in place when you are sewing the seams up.

Knit your cover...
BOTTOM PIECE OF BACK

* Using yarn doubled throughout patt and size 9 (5.5mm) needles, cast on 30 sts.
Cont in double seed stitch (UK: double moss stitch) patt.
Row 1 Inc 1 st at beg and end of row. 32 sts.
Rep this row 4 more times. 40 sts.

Cont straight until work measures 6in (15cm) from cast-on edge.*
Next row (K2, p2) to end of row.
Cont with this 2x2 rib as set until work measures 7in (17.75cm) from cast-on edge.
Bind off in patt.

The back is knitted in two separate pieces and joined with three buttons. The neck and the buttonband are made in 2x2 ribbing. Choose some buttons that will complement your choice of yarn. Here, the pearlescent buttons sit pleasingly against the lush lilac yarn.

The cute pocket allows you to keep things to hand, especially when you're feeling poorly, such as tissues, cough drops, or even some soothing lavender.

TOP PIECE OF BACK

Using yarn doubled throughout patt and size 9 (5.5mm) needles, cast on 40 sts.

Row 1 (K2, p2) to end of row.

Row 2 Cont with 2x2 rib as set.

Row 3 K2, p2, k2, p2, bind off 2 sts, p2, k2, p2, k2, p2, bind off 2 sts, p2, k2, p2, k2, p2, bind off 2 sts, p2, k2, p2. (This row sets up buttonholes.)

Row 4 P2, k2, p2, cast on 2 sts, p2, k2, p2, k2, p2, cast on 2 sts, p2, k2, p2, k2, p2, cast on 2 sts, p2, k2, p2, k2. (This row completes buttonholes.)

Cont in 2x2 rib as set until work measures 1in (2.5cm).

Change to double seed stitch patt until work measures 3½in (9cm) from cast-on edge.

Next row Dec 1 st at beg and end of the row.

Rep this row 4 more times. 30 sts.

Next row Bind off 5 sts, slip centre 20 sts on to a stitch holder, bind off 5 sts.

POCKET

Using yarn doubled throughout patt and size 9 (5.5mm) needles, cast on 20 sts.

Starting with a knit row, work in st st until work measures 4½in (11.5cm).

Break yarn and slip stitches onto stitch holder.

FRONT

Work as lower piece of back from * to *, but cont until work measure 7½in (19cm).

Now add the pocket:

Next row Patt 10 sts, bind off 20 sts in patt, patt 10 sts.

Next row Patt 10 sts, patt the 20 sts from the pocket stitch holder, patt 10 sts.

Cont working all 40 sts in double seed stitch until work measure 9½in (24cm).

Next row Dec 1 st at beg and end of the row.

Rep this row 4 more times. 30 sts.

Next row Bind off 5 sts, slip 20 sts on to a stitch holder, bind off 5 sts.

NECK

Rejoin yarn. Working with the held sts from the back, k2, p2 from this stitch holder, and then cont in 2x2 rib patt across the 2nd stitch holder.

Cont in set patt until work measures 3in (7.5cm).

Bind off in pattern.

The roomy neck will protect your hands when you're filling your bottle with hot water. For an extra luxurious finish, a satin ribbon tied round the neck is a simple but pretty addition, as shown on page 79.

Making up

Darn in any loose ends. Sew the pocket in place, leaving the top open. Add the popper and button to the middle top of the pocket. With the right sides facing, pin the front and backs together then back-stitch the seam together. Turn the right way out and sew buttons in place.

This matching hot-water
bottle is the perfect
accompaniment to the
bedsocks, and is great
when you want some extra
warmth or just a big cuddle.

Tiny tootsies...

Super-cutie bootees

Baby bootees are always a winner when you want to up the cute quotient of your knitting. They're quick to knit, colourful and fun. If your personal style is classic rather than kitsch, get in touch with your inner child by knitting these delightfully inventive bootees for your own bundle of joy or for a baby-shower gift.

  Intermediate

Measurements

To fit one-year-old child; bootee measures 5in (17.75cm) long

Gather together...

MATERIALS
A 1 x 1¾oz (50g) ball of light-weight (DK) wool, acrylic and nylon mix yarn in black

B 1 x 1¾oz (50g) ball of light-weight (DK) wool, acrylic and nylon mix yarn in yellow

NEEDLES AND NOTIONS
1 pair of size 5 (3.75mm) needles
Tapestry needle

Gauge

20 sts and 32 rows to 4in (10cm) square measured over st st using size 5 (3.75mm) needles

Knit note

For the tiger feet colourwork, follow the chart on page 124.

Tiger feet

Here we start off with a tiger-striped version (grrr!). The tiger markings are created using the intarsia technique (see page 18). Over the page you'll find strawberry and ladybug variations.

Knit your bootees...

SOLE (RIGHT AND LEFT BOOTEES KNITTED THE SAME)
Using size 5 (3.75mm) needles, cast on 6 sts using yarn A.
Row 1 K.
Row 2 K1, inc 1 st, k to last 2 sts, inc 1 st, k1. 8 sts.

Rep these 2 rows until you have 16 sts.
Cont working in garter stitch (every row k) until work measures 3½in (9cm).
Next row Dec 1 st at end of row.
Next row K.

The tiger stripe details on these bootees are created using the intarsia technique (see page 18). Weave in the loose ends as you go. The cuffs are ribbed for a snug fit, but are stretchy so will be easy to get on and off the baby.

tip

When working from a chart, be aware that each square represents a single stitch. Reading the pattern from right to left, the odd rows are knit stitches; the even rows, reading left to right, are purl stitches.

Dec 1 st at beg of every alt row until 11 sts rem.

Dec 1 st at both ends of next and following rows until 5 sts rem.

TOE OF LEFT BOOTEE

(Use chart on page 124 for reference)

** Next row K.

Next row P.

Next row Inc 1 st into each of next 4

sts, k1. 9 sts.

Next row P.

Next row K1, inc 1 st into each of next 3 sts, k to last 2 sts, inc 1, k1. 13 sts.

Rep last 2 rows until you have 25 sts.

TOE OF RIGHT BOOTEE

(Use chart on page 124 for reference)

** Next row K.

Next row P.

Next row Inc 1 st into each of next 4 sts, k1. 9 sts.

Next row P.

Next row K1, inc 1, k to the last 4 sts, inc 1 st into each of next 3 sts, k1. 13 sts.

Rep last 2 rows until you have 25 sts.

UPPER OF BOTH BOOTEES

Cont on these 25 sts until work measures 2½in (6.5cm) from **.

Next row (RS) K10, bind off 5 sts, k10.

Working on these 10 sts only:

Next row P.

Next row K1, k2tog, k to end of row.

Rep these last 2 rows until you have 7 sts.

Cont on these 7 sts until work measures 2½in (6.5cm) from the 5 bound-off sts.

Bind off.

Rejoin yarn and rep shaping for other side.

CUFF

Pick up and knit 43 sts from the ankle edge using yarn B.

Next row K1, p1 to end of row.

Next row Cont in 1x1 rib following the striped pattern as follows:

3 rows yarn B.

1 row yarn A.

3 rows yarn B.

Bind off in rib pattern in yarn B.

Making up

With right sides facing, sew seam and back. Turn the bootee the right way out and sew the top of the bootee to the sole. Darn in any loose ends.

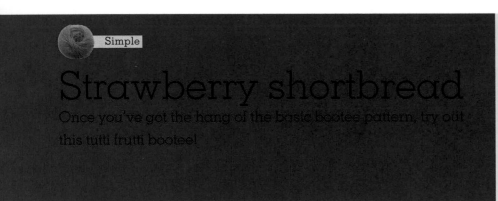

Strawberry shortbread

Once you've got the hang of the basic bootee pattern, try out this tutti frutti bootee!

MATERIALS

A 1 x 1¾oz (50g) ball of light-weight (DK) wool, acrylic and nylon mix yarn in red

B 1 x 1¾oz (50g) ball of light-weight (DK) wool, acrylic and nylon mix yarn in green

C 1 x 1¾oz (50g) ball of light-weight (DK) wool, acrylic and nylon mix yarn in yellow

27½in (70cm) of yellow ribbon ½in (1cm) wide

Knit your bootees...

Using yarn A, knit as for Tiger Feet until cuff.

CUFF

Using yarn B, pick up and knit 37 sts from ankle edge.

Cont in st st for 5 rows, starting with a purl row.

Next row (picot row) K1, *yf, k2tog, rep from * until end of row.

Cont in st st for 5 rows, starting with a purl row.

Making up

Using yarn C, swiss darn (see page 23) the strawberry seeds in place using the photograph as a guide. With right side facing, sew the back seam, then sew the top of the bootee to the sole. Fold the picot row over and sew the cuff to the top of the bootee ankle. Thread some ribbon through the cuff.

The 'pips' on these strawberry bootees are created by swiss darning over individual stitches after the bootee has been knitted. The curly leaf trim is made by a cunningly designed picot hem.

tip

When swiss darning the 'pips', weave the yarn into the wrong side as you jump from stitch to stitch. This will stop the yarn getting caught round the baby's toes.

Ladybug spots

These little bootees, complete with ladybug markings, will make your little one snug as a bug in a rug!

 Simple

MATERIALS

A 1 x 1¾oz (50g) ball of light-weight (DK) wool, acrylic and nylon mix yarn in black

B 1 x 1¾oz (50g) ball of light-weight (DK) wool, acrylic and nylon mix yarn in red

27½in (70cm) of red ribbon ½in (1cm) wide

Knit your bootees...

Knit as for Tiger Feet until cuff, using yarn A for the sole and yarn B for the top of the bootees.

CUFF

Pick up and knit 43 sts from the ankle edge using yarn A.

Cont in st st until work measures 1in (2.5cm). Fold cuff in half and sew to the bootee ankle.

Making up

Using yarn A, swiss darn (see page 23) the ladybug spots and centre stripe in place, using the photograph as a guide. With the right side facing, sew the back seam and then sew the top of the bootee to the sole. Thread some ribbon through the cuff.

The ladybug markings on this bootee are swiss darned after the bootee has been knitted. The cuff is folded in half and sewn into a place, and has a ribbon threaded through it for a cute finishing touch.

tip

Loosely tie one end of the ribbon to a safety pin and feed this through the cuff. Cut the end of the ribbon if the pin has left a hole, and tie into a small bow.

Here are some more ideas for bootees:

- **Christmas puddings** – use brown yarn with black french knots and a cream cuff with some green ribbon threaded through.
- **Soccer bootees** – use white yarn with black lines and hexagons swiss darned on top.
- **Snowflakes** – Use pretty pastel yarn with sparkly yarn embroidered on the top.

NB Don't add beads or buttons in case the baby pulls them off and tries to eat them.

Dressing-up socks

Socks don't need to be just practical garments, hidden away under shoes and trainers. With these special socks you can encourage your children's imagination by letting them play dress-up. There's a pretty pair of ballerina shoes for your little pirouetter, and a pair of lace-up soccer boots for a sport-loving child.

 Intermediate

Ballet shoes

These fanciful socks are knitted straight on two needles and then seamed up the sides. The ballet 'tight' is knitted in extra-fine merino wool, and the ballet 'shoe' in an ultra-soft polyester novelty yarn with a plush texture.

Knit your socks...

Using size 7 (4.5mm) needles and yarn A, cast on 41 sts.

Row 1 (RS) K.

Row 2 P.

Rep these 2 rows once more.

Picot edge row K2tog, *yf, k2tog, rep from * to last st, k1.

Cont in st st for 3 rows, starting with a purl row.

Next row Knit to last 2 sts, k2tog. 40 sts.

Cont in st st until the work measures 8½in (22cm).

RIGHT SOCK

Change to yarn B.

Next row K25, rejoin yarn A, k10, change back to yarn B, k5.

Cont in pattern as set for 3 more rows.

Measurements

To fit 7–8 year-old child

Gather together...

MATERIALS

A 2 x 1¾oz (50g) balls of light-weight (DK) extra fine merino wool yarn in white

B 1 x 1¾oz (50g) ball of light-weight (DK) polyester yarn in pink

NEEDLES AND NOTIONS

1 pair of size 7 (4.5mm) needles
Stitch marker
3ft (1m) of pink ric-rac trimming
6ft (2m) of pink satin ribbon

Gauge

20 sts and 24 rows to 4in (10cm) measured over st st using size 7 (4.5mm) needles

A pretty picot trim runs around the cuff of these socks, while ric-rac trimmings and a pink satin ribbon add some authentic ballerina-style touches.

LEFT SOCK

Change to yarn B.

Next row K5, rejoin yarn A, k10, change back to yarn B, k25.

Cont in pattern as set for 4 more rows.

SHAPE RIGHT HEEL

Next row K20, turn.

Next row P18, yf, sl 1, yb, turn.

Next row Sl 1, k17, yf, sl 1, yb, turn.

Next row Sl 1, p16, yf, sl 1, yb, turn.

Cont in this way until 8 sts have been worked.

Next row K9, turn.

Next row P10, turn.

Cont in this way until all heel sts have been worked.

SHAPE LEFT HEEL

Next row P20, turn.

Next row K18, yf, sl 1, yb, turn.

Next row Sl 1, p17, yf, sl 1, yb, turn.

Next row Sl 1, k16, yf, sl 1, yb, turn.

Cont in this way until 8 sts have been worked.

Next row P9, turn

Next row K10, turn.

Cont in this way until all heel sts have been worked.

Soccer boots

These sporty socks are knitted in two shades of merino wool, complete with laces for an authentic soccer-boot look. The cuff is ribbed to help the socks stay up.

The ric-rac trimming is sewn around the edge of the pink fabric to distinguish the pink 'shoe' from the white 'tight'. The pink section is worked in stockinette stitch, just like the white section, although the brushed texture of the yarn means that you won't be able to see this stitch definition.

BOTH SOCKS

Cont across all sts in pattern as set until the work measures 4¾in (12cm) from the heel, ending with a purl row.

RIGHT FOOT

Next row K26 in yarn B, k8 in yarn A, k6 in yarn B.

Next row P7 in yarn B, p6 in yarn A, p27 in yarn B.

Next row K28 in yarn B, k4 in yarn A, k8 in yarn B.

Next row P all sts in yarn B.

LEFT FOOT

Next row K6 in yarn B, k8 in yarn A, k26 in yarn B.

Next row P27 in yarn B, p6 in yarn A, p7 in yarn B.

Next row K8 in yarn B, k4 in yarn A, k28 in yarn B.

Next row P all sts in yarn B.

BOTH FEET

**Cont in yarn B for 4 more rows (or to the desired length), placing a stitch marker at the centre of the row.

TOE

Next row K1, k2tog, k to 3 sts before the marker, k2tog, k2, k2tog, k to last 3 sts, k2tog, k1. 36 sts.

Next row P1, p2tog, p to 3 sts before the marker, p2tog, p2, p2tog, p to last 3 sts, p2tog, p1. 32 sts.

Rep these last 2 rows until 8 sts rem. Bind off.

Making up

Darn in any loose ends.

Cut the ric rac in half. With a matching cotton thread stitch the ric rac around the edge of pink yarn of the foot (use the photograph as a guide).

Cut the satin ribbon in half, fold the ribbon in half and stitch to the middle of the heel.

Stitch the side seam of the sock together, fold over the picot edge and sew into place.

Measurements

To fit 7–8 year-old child

Gather together...

MATERIALS

A 2 x 1¾oz (50g) balls of light-weight (DK) extra fine merino wool yarn in white

B 1 x 1¾oz (50g) balls of light-weight (DK) extra fine merino wool yarn in blue

Oddment of black yarn for embellishments

NEEDLES AND NOTIONS

1 pair of size 7 (4.5mm) needles
1 size E4 (3.50mm) crochet hook
2 bootlaces or ribbon ties

Gauge

20 sts and 24 rows to 4in (10cm) measured over st st using size 7 (4.5mm) needles

These sporty socks are made in crisp blue and white merino wool – nice and warm for when your child is running about!

Knit your socks...

Cast on 40 sts using size 7 (4.5mm) needles and yarn A.

Next row K2, p2 to end of row.

Cont in 2x2 rib for 5 more rows.

Cont in st st until the work measures 6¼in (16cm). Change to yarn B and work for further 1½in (4cm).

RIGHT SOCK

Change to yarn A and complete the heel as for right Ballet shoe. After finishing the heel, rejoin yarn B,

working 20 sts with yarn A and 20 sts with yarn B.

LEFT SOCK

Next row K20 sts in yarn B, change to yarn A and k20.

Complete heel as for left Ballet shoe. After finishing the heel, rejoin yarn B, working 20 sts with yarn A and 20 sts with yarn B.

BOTH SOCKS

Complete the sock as for Ballet shoes from **.

Making up

Darn in all loose ends. With E4 (3.50mm) crochet hook and black yarn, chain stitch through sock from the start of the toe shaping, round the heel of the sock and to the start of the toe shaping on the other side of the foot. With E4 (3.50mm) crochet hook and yarn A, chain stitch 2 columns up from the toe section to the edge of the blue knitting to show the trainer's tongue section (see photograph for reference). Add bootlace or ribbon tie as in the photograph.

Fairy socks

These prettily embellished pastel-coloured socks will make any little girl feel like a fairy princess. Knitted in fine-weight (4ply) yarn with delicate hand-stitched decorations, these socks make a lovely keepsake. The socks are knitted in the round, and the colourwork is done in intarsia (see page 18) and embroidery. The chart for the colourwork can be found on page 124.

Advanced

Measurements

To fit ages 2–3 [4–5: 5–6: 7–8]

Gather together...

MATERIALS

A 1 x 1¾oz (50g) ball of fine-weight (4ply) merino wool in pale blue

B 1 x 1¾oz (50g) ball of fine-weight (4ply) merino wool in rose pink

C 1 x 1¾oz (50g) ball of fine-weight (4ply) merino wool in pale pink

D 1 x 1¾oz (50g) ball of fine-weight (4ply) merino wool in sage green

E 1 x 1¾oz (50g) ball of fine-weight (4ply) merino wool in pale yellow

NEEDLES AND NOTIONS

1 set of size 1 (2.5mm) double-pointed needles
Butterfly wing embellishments
Stitch marker

Gauge

32 sts and 44 rows to 4in (10cm) square measured over st st using size 1 (2.5mm) needles

Knit your socks...

Cast on 32 [36: 40: 44] sts using yarn A and size 1 (2.5mm) double-pointed needles. Divide sts over 3 needles, placing a marker to show beg of round.

Work a k1, p1 rib for 12 rounds.

Change to yarn B and knit 6 [6: 8: 8] rounds.

Change to yarn C and knit 3 [3: 4: 4] rounds.

Change to yarn B and knit 6 [6: 8: 8] rounds.

Change to yarn A and knit 4 [5: 6: 7] rounds.

FOR RIGHT SOCK

Next round K7 [8: 9: 10] sts and place chart A (see page 124), starting from the top of the head and working downwards until 4th-to-last row. Then continue chart while following hill pattern below.

FOR LEFT SOCK

Next round K23 [26: 29: 32] sts and place chart B (see page 124), starting from the top of the head and working downwards until 4th-to-last row. Then continue chart while following hill pattern below.

HILL PATTERN

Round 1 of hill pattern Starting from edge of fairy skirt, k3 with yarn A, k3 with yarn D to the next row of chart.

Round 2 of hill pattern Starting from edge of fairy skirt, k1 with yarn D, k1 with yarn A, k5 with yarn D to the next row of chart.

Round 3 of hill pattern K every st with yarn D until next row of chart.

Cont with yarn D until all rows of chart pattern are complete for 2 [3: 4: 5] rounds.

Socks are a great project for colourwork, as all the scrappy yarn ends from changing colours are tucked away on the inside. Here we've used four pretty soft-toned colours worked in blocks as the backdrop for the fairy figures. The basic shapes of the fairies, and the hilly backdrop they are set against, are worked in intarsia, while the details are hand-embroidered afterwards.

HEEL FLAP

K first 8 [9: 10: 11] sts onto 1 needle. K next 16 [18: 20: 22] sts onto 2nd needle. Then k final 8 [9: 10: 11] sts onto 1st needle.

Working on just the 1st needle, turn, slip 1, P to end.

Next row Sl 1, k to end of row.

Next row Sl 1, p to end of row.

Rep last 2 rows 10 [11: 12: 13] more times.

SHAPE HEEL

Sl 1, k9 [10:11: 12], ssk, k1, turn.

Sl 1, p5, p2tog, p1, turn.

Sl 1, k6, ssk, k1, turn.

Sl 1, p8 p2tog, p1, turn.

Sl 1, k9, ssk, k1, turn.

Cont in this way until 10 [12: 14: 16] sts rem, ending on a purl row.

GUSSET

Now it's time to pick up sts.

With spare needle, knit 5 [6: 7: 8] sts from the heel needle.

Needle 1 K next 5 [6: 7: 8] sts, then pick up and knit 11 [12: 13: 14] sts from the side of the heel.

Needle 2 K across all 16 [18: 20: 22] sts.

Needle 3 Pick up and knit 11 [12: 13: 14] sts from side of heel and k across 5 [6: 7: 8] sts on spare needle. 48 [54: 60: 66] sts.

Simple embroidery stitches, clever choice of colours, and the addition of some shop-bought sparkling butterfly wings bring the little fairy figures to life.

SHAPE GUSSET

Round 1

Needle 1 Knit to last 3 sts, k2tog, k1.

Needle 2 K.

Needle 3 K1, ssk, knit to end of
 needle.

Round 2

Knit all three needles.

Rep last 2 rounds until:

Needle 1 8 [9: 10: 11] sts rem.

Needle 2 16 [18: 20: 22] sts.

Needle 3 8 [9: 10: 11] sts rem.

FOOT

Now knit every round until sock from
 start of heel shaping measures 1½in
 (4cm) less than required foot length.

SHAPE TOE

Round 1

Needle 1 K to last 3 sts, k2tog, k1.

Needle 2 K1, ssk, k to last 3 sts,
 k2tog, k1.

Needle 3 k1, ssk, k to end of needle.

Round 2

K.

Rep last 2 rounds until a total of 14
 [16: 18: 20] sts rem. Work across
 sts on needle 1. Place rem sts onto
 2 needles, then graft the toe (see
 page 21).

Making up

Darn in any loose ends.
Using photographs as a guide,
embroider the fairy's hair using yarn
E. Embroider hair bands using yarn B.
Embroider legs and arms using yarn
C. Embroider shoes using yarn A.
Sew on butterfly embellishments
using invisible sewing thread.
Alternatively, you could embroider
wings using yarn E.

tip *If you're not
confident enough
to attempt
intarsia, just
follow the pattern
without placing the charts.
This will give you a great
background to embroider
on, or to sew on fairy
embellishments.*

This close-up of one of the fairies shows
you how effective and expressive a few
simple embroidery stitches can be.

Secret-keeper socks

Children will love these chunky socks – partly because of their cheerful colours, but mostly because of their special pocket – complete with snap fasteners to keep all their secret things safe and hidden.

 Simple

Jungle explorer socks

These socks are made in a wonderful variegated yarn, so you get fantastic colour effects with minimal effort. The pocket is made in a complementary solid shade. These socks are knitted straight on two needles and seamed together afterwards.

Special instruction

The pocket flap is worked in seed stitch (UK: moss stitch). K1, p1 for the first row. Then purl the knits and knit the purls on the way back. This creates quite a bumpy-looking fabric with lots of texture.

Measurements

To fit 9–10-year old child

Gather together...

MATERIALS
A 2 x 1¾oz (50g) balls of medium-weight (aran) alpaca and wool mix yarn in variegated green, brown and navy
B 1 x 1¾oz (50g) ball of medium-weight (aran) alpaca and wool mix yarn in chartreuse green

NEEDLES AND NOTIONS
1 pair of size 9 (5.5mm) needles
2 stitch holders
4 snap fasteners

Gauge

17 sts and 22 rows to 4in (10cm) measured over st st using size 9 (5.5 mm) needles

The variegated yarn used for these socks creates colour effects reminiscent of camouflage patterns – perfect for your little jungle explorer!

Knit your socks...

POCKETS
(Make 2)

Using size 9 (5.5mm) needles, cast on 12 sts in yarn B.

Work in st st for 12 rows.

Slip these sts on to a stitch holder.

Using size 9 (5.5mm) needles, cast on 36 sts using yarn A.

Row 1 K1, p1 to the end of row.

Cont with 1x1 rib for 4 rows.

Row 6 K.

Row 7 P.

The last 2 rows form st st. Cont in st st for 12 more rows.

Next row K12, join pocket by knitting the pocket stitches and the next 12

stitches together, k12.

Next row P12.

POCKET FLAP

Rejoin yarn B and work in seed stitch (UK: moss stitch) for 4 rows. Then bind off these 12 sts.

Rejoin yarn A and p12.

Next row K12, cast on 12 sts, k12.

Next row P.

Next row K.

Cont in st st until the work measures 8½in (22cm) from the cast-on edge.

SHAPE RIGHT HEEL

Next row K18, turn.

Next row Sl 1, p16 yf, sl 1, yb, turn.

Next row Sl 1, k15, yf, sl 1, yb, turn.

Next row Sl 1, P14, yf, sl 1, yb, turn.

Cont in this way until 8 sts have been worked.

Next row K9, turn.

Next row P10, turn.

Cont in this way until all heel sts have been worked.

SHAPE LEFT HEEL

Next row P18, turn.

Next row Sl 1, k16, yf, sl 1, yb, turn.

Next row Sl 1, p15, yf, sl 1, yb, turn.

Next row Sl 1, k14, yf, sl 1, yb, turn.

Cont in this way until 8 sts have been worked.

Next row P9, turn

Next row K10, turn.

Cont in this way until all heel sts have been worked.

BOTH SOCKS

Cont across all sts with the pattern as set until the work measures 5in (12.5cm) or desired length from heel, ending with a purl row and placing a stitch marker at the centre of the row.

TOE

Next row K1, k2tog, k to 3 sts before the marker, k2tog, k2, k2tog, k to last 3 sts, k2tog, k1. 32 sts.

Next row P1, p2tog, p to 3 sts before the marker, p2tog, p2, p2tog, p to last 3 sts, p2tog, p1. 28 sts.

Rep these last 2 rows until 8 sts rem. Bind off.

Making up

Darn in any loose ends. Stitch in the pocket and the side seams. With a matching thread, sew 2 snap fasteners in place on the pocket flap and 2 on the pocket top.

Simple

Pink pockets

This sweet pink version of the secret-keeper socks is made for a slightly younger child. Here, the pocket is picked out in a pretty purple yarn.

Measurements

To fit 7–8-year-old child

Gather together...

MATERIALS

A 2 x 1¾oz (50g) balls of light-weight (DK) wool yarn in pink

B 1 x 1¾oz (50g) ball of light-weight (DK) wool yarn in purple

NEEDLES AND NOTIONS

1 pair of size 7 (4.5mm) needles

2 stitch holders

2 snap fasteners

Gauge

22 sts and 28 rows to 4in (10cm) measured over st st using size 7 (4.5mm) needles

This fun pocket is perfect for keeping special things in. Attach some snap fasteners so the pocket can be closed up to keep treasures safe and hidden.

This version is knitted to the same basic pattern as the Jungle Explorer Socks, but uses a lighter weight of yarn and smaller needles, so the finished item will be smaller and therefore fit a younger child.

Knit your socks...

Make 2 pockets as for Jungle Explorer socks but using size 7 (4.5mm) needles instead of size 9 (5.5mm) needles.

Using size 7 (4.5mm) needles, cast on 72 sts in yarn A.
Work 2 rows of st st.
Next row K2tog to end of row. 36 sts.
Next row P.

Cont as for Jungle Explorer socks until the pocket flap, then cont for flap as follows using yarn B:
Next row K12.
Next row P2tog, p10, p2tog.
Next row K2tog, k8, k2tog.
Next row P2tog, p6, p2tog.
Bind off.

Cont as for Jungle Explorer socks.

Pirate socks

These bright and bold striped socks, complete with felt skull and crossbones, will bring out the pirate in your kids when they're in the mood for some swashbuckling adventures. Parrot and pieces of eight not included...

Knit your socks...

Using size 7 (4.5mm) needles, cast on 40 sts using yarn A.

Row 1 (RS) K1, p2, *k2, p2; rep from * to last st, k1.

Row 2 P1, k2, *p2, k2; rep from * to last st, p1.

Rep these 2 rows 6 more times.

Change to yarn B and cont in st st, starting with a knit row.

Changing yarns every 6 rows to work in six-row stripes, cont in st st for 36 rows (3 black stripes and 3 red stripes worked).

Change to yarn B and work 2 rows in st st.

SHAPE RIGHT HEEL

Next row K20, turn.

Next row P18, yf, sl 1, yb, turn.

Next row Sl 1, k17, yf, sl 1, yb, turn.

Next row Sl 1, P16, yf, sl 1, yb, turn.

Cont in this way until 8 sts have been worked.

Next row K9, turn.

Next row P10, turn.

Cont in this way until all heel sts have been worked.

SHAPE LEFT HEEL

Next row K.

Next row P20, turn.

Next row K18, yf, sl 1, yb, turn.

Next row Sl 1, p17, yf, sl 1, yb, turn.

Next row Sl 1, k16, yf, sl 1, yb, turn.

Cont in this way until 8 sts have been worked.

Next row P9, turn.

Next row K10, turn.

Cont in this way until all heel sts have been worked.

The skull and crossbones are made out of pieces of white and black felt. Use the photograph as a template if your freehand drawing skills aren't quite up to the job. Draw the mouth on with a fabric marker pen.

Simple

Measurements

To fit 7–8-year-old child

Gather together...

MATERIALS

A 1 x 3½oz (100g) ball of light-weight (DK) acrylic yarn in bright red

B 1 x 3½oz (100g) ball of light-weight (DK) acrylic yarn in black

NEEDLES AND NOTIONS

1 pair of size 7 (4.5mm) needles

White felt and black felt

Black fabric pen

Gauge

20 sts and 24 rows to 4in (10cm) measured over st st using size 7 (4.5mm) needles

These vividly colourful pirate socks are perfect for a dressing-up day or for Halloween – or for whenever your child is in the mood for adventure! The socks are knitted straight on two needles and seamed up the sides afterwards. The yarn is a hard-wearing acrylic.

BOTH SOCKS

Cont across all sts with the pattern as set until the work measures 4¾in (12cm) from the heel or desired length, ending with a purl row and placing a stitch marker at the centre of the row.

TOE

Next row K1, k2tog, k to 3 sts before the marker, k2tog, k2, k2tog, k to last 3 sts, k2tog, k1. 36 sts.

Next row P1, p2tog, p to 3 sts before the marker, p2tog, p2, p2tog, p to last 3 sts, p2tog, p1. 32 sts.

Rep these last 2 rows until 8 sts rem. Bind off.

Making up

Darn in any loose ends. With the white felt, cut out 2 skull and 8 bone shapes. Stitch or glue them into place. With the black felt, cut out 4 black circles for the eyes and stitch or glue them into place. Draw on a mouth with a black fabric pen. Sew up the side seams.

Think outside the socks...

Peep-toe pedicure

Now you see them...now you paint! These ingenious socks solve a dilemma that every glamour girl faces some time – how do you keep your pedicure salon-fabulous when your feet are freezing? Answer – a snap-on, snap-off toe so you can polish your paintwork but keep the rest of your foot woolly warm! These socks are knitted in the round from the heel to the ball of the foot. The toe section is made separately, with the back part sewn to the underside of the sock and the front part fixed by poppers. We've made a vibrant self-striping pair – no yarn-changing hassle – and a pair in bright orange and green.

  | Intermediate

Measurements

One size fits all

Gather together...

MATERIALS
1 x 5¼oz (150g) hank of light-weight (DK) pure alpaca yarn in variegated red, orange and green

NEEDLES AND NOTIONS
1 set of size 6 (4mm) double-pointed needles
1 set of size 4 (3.5mm) double-pointed needles
4 snap fasteners
Stitch markers

Gauge

24 sts and 36 rows to 4in (10cm) square measured over st st using size 4 (3.5mm) needles

Knit your socks...

(Make 2)
**Using size 6 (4mm) needles, cast on 44 sts and divide them over 3 needles. Add a stitch marker to mark the start of the round.
Round 1 K2, p2; rep for round.
Cont in 2x2 rib as set until you have completed 10 rounds.
Round 11 Change to size 4 (3.5mm) needles and cont with knit stitch** until work measures 3in (7.5cm) from cast-on edge.

HEEL FLAP
Next row K11, turn.
Next row P22.
Work straight on these 22 sts for 22 rows.

SHAPE HEEL
Next row K13 sts, ssk, k1, turn.
Next row P5, p2tog, p1, turn.
Next row K to st before gap, ssk, k1, turn.
Next row P to st before gap, p2tog, p1, turn.
Rep these last 2 rows until 14 sts rem, ending on a purl row.
Next row K.

With these clever socks, there's no reason to forego your pedicure pampering when it's too chilly to be barefoot. A popper fastening allows you to open the socks so that just your toes are revealed, ready for some beauty treatment.

These socks are made from pure alpaca yarn, which makes a particularly warm fabric. The variegated yarn is dyed in wonderfully vibrant colours.

GUSSET

Next row Pick up and knit 12 sts from side of heel, placing stitch marker after last st.

K 22 sts from next needle.

With 3rd needle, pick up and knit 12 sts from side of heel, placing stitch marker before 1st st, k6, k1 from next needle.

SHAPE GUSSET

Round 1 K to 3 sts before stitch marker, k2tog, k1, slip stitch marker, knit to next stitch marker, k1, ssk, k to end of round.

Round 2 K.

Rep last 2 rounds until 44 sts.

FOOT

Cont on these sts until foot measures 6in (15cm) or desired length.

Next round K2, p2 to end of round.

Cont in 2x2 rib as set until you have completed 10 rounds.

Bind off in rib patt.

SHAPE TOE

Work as from ** to ** then cont in knit until toe measures 2½in (6cm).

Round 1 Knit to 3 sts before 1st stitch marker, k2tog, k1, slip marker, k1, ssk, knit to 3 sts before next marker, k2tog, k1, slip marker, k1, ssk, k to end of round.

Round 2 K.

Cont to work decs in this way until 20 sts rem. Then work round 1 only until 8 sts rem. Using 3-needle bind-off to join toe (see page 20).

Making up

Darn in any loose ends. Sew the back of the toe to the sole of the sock at the first rib row. Attach the 2 pop fasteners to the rib sections of the sock and the toe.

The toe is knitted separately from the main section of the sock, starting with the ribbed section and ending with the toe shaping. Use a three-needle bind-off for a seamless finish.

tip

'Ladders' can sometimes appear in knitted fabric when working in the round at the points where you change needles. To avoid this, knit a couple of stitches from the beginning of the next needle as you work. This will help to prevent laddering by moving round the point where you change needles.

Citrus blocks

The same weight of yarn is used for this block version (opposite) so the pattern instructions are exactly the same as for the stripy version.

MATERIALS

2 x 1¾oz (50g) balls of light-weight (DK) wool, acrylic and polyamide mix yarn in orange

1 x 1¾oz (50g) ball of light-weight (DK) wool, acrylic and polyamide mix yarn in green

Five-toe stripy socks

These delightful socks combine traditional tweedy elegance with a lively twist. It might seem a bit eccentric to knit each toe individually, but just think of these socks as gloves for your feet. They'll certainly keep your toes warm! These socks are knitted in the round using light-weight (DK) tweed yarn. We've gone for simple stripes, but you could vary the pattern by knitting each toe in a separate colour. These socks would make a great follow-on project from the Around and Around Socks (pages 28–31), if you're fairly new to knitting on double-pointed needles and want to push your skills a stage further.

 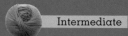
Intermediate

Measurements

One size fits all

Gather together...

MATERIALS

A 1 x 1¾oz (50g) ball of light-weight (DK) acrylic, cotton and wool mix tweed yarn in brown

B 1 x 1¾oz (50g) ball of light-weight (DK) acrylic, cotton and wool mix tweed yarn in cream

C 1 x 1¾oz (50g) ball of light-weight (DK) acrylic, cotton and wool mix tweed yarn in blue

NEEDLES AND NOTIONS

1 set of size 6 (4mm) double-pointed needles

Stitch marker

3 stitch holders or safety pins

Gauge

Achieving an exact gauge is not essential for this project because the ribbing makes the knitted fabric stretchy

Knit your socks...

(Make 2)

Using size 6 (4mm) double-pointed needles, cast on 50 sts using yarn A. Mark beg of round with stitch marker.

Round 1 K3, p2 to end of round.

Cont 3x2 rib throughout patt, changing colour every 16 rows until desired length. We did 2 stripes each in yarns A, B and C.

BIG TOE

Next round Rejoin yarn A, k7, slip next 36 sts on to stitch holders, cast on 4 sts, k7. 18 sts.

Next round K.

Cont on these sts until toe measures 2in (5cm).

K2tog until you have 3 sts, break yarn and thread through sts, pull tight and fasten off.

Ribbing is a great stitch to use for knitted socks because the stretchy nature of the fabric means you'll get a good fit with minimal effort and shaping. We've knitted the socks in thick stripes using three shades of tweed yarn in warm, earthy colours. The flecks of colour in the yarn create a lovely organic-looking, rich texture.

SECOND AND THIRD TOE

Next round K5 from stitch holder, cast on 3 sts, k last 5 sts from stitch holder, pick up and knit 3 sts from big toe. 16 sts.

Next round K.

Cont in st st until toe measures 1¾in (4.5cm).

K2tog until you have 1 st remaining, then fasten off.

FOURTH TOE

Next round K4 from stitch holder, cast on 3 sts, knit last 4 sts from stitch holder, pick up and knit 3 sts from big toe. 14 sts.

Next round K.

Cont in st st until toe measures 1½in (4cm).

K2tog until you have 1 st remaining, then fasten off.

FIFTH TOE

Next round K8 from stitch holder, pick up and knit 3 sts from big toe. 11 sts.

Next round K.

Cont in st st until toe measures 1in (2.5cm).

K2tog until you have 1 st remaining, then fasten off.

Making up

Darn in any loose ends.

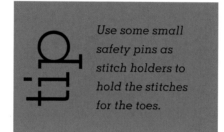

tip

Use some small safety pins as stitch holders to hold the stitches for the toes.

Knitting all the individual toes might seem difficult, but it's actually quite simple. Starting with the big toe, each toe is worked separately, with the remaining stitches held on stitch holders until you need them. You simply cast on a few stitches to complete the round for each toe, and then knit in the round, decreasing at the top to create the curved shape for the tip of the toe.

Giving your dad socks for Christmas is as traditional as turkey and stuffing. This time, however, make sure he gets something really special. Hand-knitted socks are much more thoughtful than shop-bought ones, and this quirky twist on the traditional sock is sure to make him laugh – while also keeping his toes toasty!

Luscious legwarmers

Legwarmers are always a fun way to introduce a playful, kitschy retro twist into your look, and they're great fun to make too. They also have a practical element, giving you that extra bit of warmth when cosy socks aren't quite enough to stave off the chills. We've offered you two great-looking options here; one with a wonderful cable and bobble pattern, and a flared pair in a pretty variegated yarn. Both of these pairs of legwarmers are knitted straight on two needles.

Loveheart legwarmers

These legwarmers are made in a sturdy, tweedy cream-coloured yarn reminiscent of traditional aran jumpers and ganseys – a look that is reinforced by the deeply textured pattern of heart-shaped cables and bobbles. These legwarmers are knitted straight on two needles from the ankle to the calf. They are shaped partly by increases and partly by changing to a larger size of needle once the first cable section has been completed.

The textural detail of the heart-shaped cable pattern and the funky bobbles stand out superbly against the thick oatmeal-coloured tweedy yarn.

Measurements

One size fits all; overall length is 13¾in (35cm)

Gather together...

MATERIALS
2 x 3½oz (100g) balls of medium-weight (aran) 100% wool in cream tweed

NEEDLES AND NOTIONS
1 pair of size 7 (4.5mm) needles
1 pair of size 9 (5.5mm) needles
Cable needle
Stitch markers

Gauge

16 sts and 23 rows to 4in (10cm) square measured over st st using size 9 (5.5mm) needles

tip

If you have very slender legs, try knitting some elastic into the top rib. You can make the legwarmers longer or shorter by knitting more or fewer repeats of the cable pattern.

Special abbreviations

(Note: pay special attention to whether the abbreviation is lowercase or uppercase – C2b is different from C2B!)

C2b Sl 1 st onto cable needle and hold at back, k1, p st from cable needle

C2B Sl 1 st onto cable needle and hold at back, k1, k st from cable needle

C2f Sl 1 st onto cable needle and hold at front, p1, k st from cable needle

C2F Sl 1 st onto cable needle and hold at front, k1, k st from cable needle

C3b Sl 1 st onto cable needle and hold at back, k2, p st from cable needle

C3f Sl 2 sts onto cable needle and hold at front, p1, k2 sts from cable needle

C4F Place next 2 sts onto cable needle and hold at front of work, k2, then k sts from cable needle

Knit your legwarmers...

(Make 2)

HEART CABLE PATTERN

Row 1 WS facing, k6, p4, k6.
Row 2 P6, C4F, p6.
Row 3 K6, p4, k6.
Row 4 P5, C3b, C3f, p5.
Row 5 K5, p2, k2, p2, k5.
Row 6 P4, C3b, p2, C3f, p4.
Row 7 K4, p2, k4, p2, k4.
Row 8 P3, C3b, p4, C3f, p3.
Row 9 K3, p2, k6, p2, k3.
Row 10 P2, C3b, C3b, C3f, C3f, p2.
Row 11 K2, (p2, k1, p2, k2) twice.
Row 12 P1, C3b, C3b, p2, C3f, C3f, p1.
Row 13 (K1, p2) twice, k4, (p2, k1) twice.
Row 14 P1, k1, C2f, C3f, p2, C3b, C2b, k1, p1.
Row 15 (K1, p1) twice, k1, p2, k2, p2, k1, (p1, k1) twice.
Row 16 P1, k1, p1, C2f, C3f, C3b, C2b, p1, k1, p1.
Row 17 K1, p1, k2, p1, k1, p4, k1, p1, k2, p1, k1.
Row 18 P1, C2f, C2b, p1, C4F, p1, C2f, C2b, p1.
Row 19 K2, C2B, k2, p4, k2, C2F, k2.
Rep from row 4.

The bobble pattern makes a fantastically textural, three-dimensional stitch that stands out against the backdrop of reverse stockinette stitch.

BOBBLE PATTERN

P to stitch, (yo, k1) 3 times into the same st.
Turn, sl1 purlwise, p5.
Turn, sl1 knitwise, k5.
Turn, p2tog 3 times.
Turn, sl1 knitwise, k2tog, psso.
Carry on with rest of row as set.

LEGWARMERS

Cast on 42 sts using size 7 (4.5mm) needles.
Work a k1, p1 rib for 1½in (4cm).
Next row Still working in rib pattern, evenly inc 14 sts across row. 56 sts.
Next row Still working in rib pattern, evenly inc 12 sts across row. 68 sts.

Working cables always looks complicated (and very impressive!), but they are actually far simpler than they might seem. Just read the pattern carefully, and mark the beginning and end of the pattern section with stitch markers so you know exactly where to make the twists.

tip

Using stitch markers along the row helps you to know where to start and end the cable pattern.

Cable pattern starts:

Row 1 K3, place 16 st heart pattern, pm, k7, pm, place 16 st heart pattern, pm, k7, pm, place 16 st heart pattern, k3.

Now with heart pattern set, every 6th row of pattern add a bobble to the 4th st of the 2 sections of 7 sts.

After first heart pattern has been competed to row 19, change to size 9 (5.5mm) needles.

Work heart and bobble pattern 3 more times.

Next row P, decreasing 12 sts evenly along row. 56 sts.

Next row Work k1, p1 rib.

Cont in k1, p1 rib until rib section measures 1½in (4cm).

Bind off in rib.

Making up

Darn in any loose ends. Sew up the back seam, using a reverse st st mattress stitch to make the seam flat.

Bell-bottomed beauties

Simple

These shorter-length legwarmers are flared for a full-on retro vibe. We've made them in some beautiful variegated hand-dyed yarn, so the 'stripes' make themselves. These legwarmers are simple to make by knitting straight on two needles.

Measurements

One size fits all; with the cuff folded down the legwarmers are approximately 9in (23cm) long.

Gather together...

MATERIALS
2 x 1¾oz (50g) balls of medium-weight (aran) silk, kid mohair and lambswool mix yarn in variegated purples, blues and browns

NEEDLES AND NOTIONS
1 pair of size 9 (5.5mm) needles

Gauge

16 sts and 20 rows to 4in (10cm) square measured over st st using size 9 (5.5mm) needles

Knit your legwarmers...

(Make 2)

Using size 9 (5.5mm) needles, cast on 48 sts.
Row 1 K1, p2, *k2, p2; rep from * to last st, k1.
Row 2 P1, k2, *p2, k2; rep from * to last st, p1.
Cont in the 2x2 rib as set until work measures 5in (13cm).
Next row K.
Next row P.
These 2 rows form st st.
Cont in st st, increasing 4 sts evenly on row 13 and then on every following 4th row until 76 sts.
Cont on these sts for a further 3 rows.
Cont in 2x2 rib as for the top cuff of the legwarmers for 5 rows.
Bind off in rib pattern.

Making up
Darn in any loose ends, and sew up the seams.

The ribbed section at the top of the legwarmers will help them to stay up without sagging.

To make a longer legwarmer, simply knit to the required length before working the increases.

These legwarmers are knitted in beautiful hand-dyed yarn. You won't get distinct stripes with this yarn, but lovely colour effects as one shade merges into the next. Note that each yarn is unique, so your two legwarmers are unlikely to match each other exactly.

Silky split-toe socks

These cute socks are reminiscent of the traditional Japanese split-toe socks called *tabi* that were worn with kimonos. Updated versions of the style are still hugely popular in Japan today. We've embellished our take on the socks with crocheted circles in toning colours. The socks are knitted in the round using standard light-weight (DK) yarn. The cuff is made in stockinette stitch; this will automatically roll over at the top so that the wrong side shows.

  Intermediate

Measurements

One size fits all

Gather together...

MATERIALS

2 x 1¾oz (50g) balls of light-weight (DK) bamboo and wool mix yarn in pink

Oddments of light-weight (DK) yarn in 4 pastel colours for embellishments

NEEDLES AND NOTIONS

1 set of size 5 (3.75mm) double-pointed needles
1 size E4 (3.50mm) crochet hook
Stitch marker
Stitch holder

Gauge

22 sts and 28 rows to 4in (10cm) square measured over st st using size 5 (3.75mm) needles

Knit your socks...

**Using size 5 (3.75mm) double-pointed needles, cast on 48 sts and divide between 3 needles. Place stitch marker to mark beg of round.
Knit every row until work measures 4in (10cm).

HEEL FLAP

Next row K22, yf, sl1, yb, turn.
Next row Sl 1, p20, yf, sl 1, yb, turn.
Next row Sl 1, k19, yf, sl 1, yb, turn.
Next row Sl 1, p18, yf, sl 1, yb, turn.
Cont in this way until 10 sts have been worked.

SHAPE HEEL AND GUSSET

Next row K9, turn.
Next row P10, turn.
Cont in this way until all the heel sts have been worked.

GUSSET AND FOOT

Knit each round until work measures 6½in (16.5cm), or desired length for foot.

BIG TOE OF RIGHT FOOT

Next round K7, slip next 34 sts on to stitch holder, cast on 4 sts, k7. 18 sts.
Next round K.
Cont on these sts until toe measures 2in (5cm).

You're sure to turn heads in these daringly different socks, so show off your take on the *tabi* with a funky pair of flip-flops.

K2tog until you have 3 sts. Break yarn and thread through rem sts, pull tight and fasten off.

TOES (SAME FOR BOTH FEET)

Knit the sts from the stitch holder, adding a stitch marker to mark beg of round, then pick up and knit the 4 sts from the big toe. 38 sts.

Next round K14, k2tog, k2, k2tog, k18. 36 sts.

Next round K.

Next round K13, k2tog, k2, k2tog, k17. 34 sts.

Next round K.

Cont to decrease as above until 16 sts rem.

Next round Bind off using 3-needle bind-off method (see page 20).

Once the main part of the sock has been knitted, you work the big toe section and then the other toe section. For the big toe, you knit part way across the round, put the stitches for the other toe section on stitch holders to be worked on later, and then cast on a few stitches to fill the gap. Then knit the toe in the round, decreasing at the top to create the curved toe shape.

BIG TOE OF LEFT FOOT

Work as for big toe of right foot but begin the big toe on the right side of the foot.

CROCHETED EMBELLISHMENTS

Using E4 (3.50mm) crochet hook, ch 5 sts, sl st into the 1st ch to form a loop.

Next round Ch 2, sc 15 sts into the loop.

Fasten off.

Make 15 circles for each sock using the toning-coloured yarns.

Making up

Darn in any loose ends on the socks and crocheted circles. Attach the circles to the socks with a matching yarn.

The yarn for these socks is 80% bamboo and 20% wool. This creates a smooth and slightly floppy fabric with a softness and sheen reminiscent of silk yarn. We've added crocheted circles in toning colours to embellish the soft lilac-pink of the main sock.

ALTERNATIVE STAR EMBELLISHMENTS

Using E4 (3.50mm) crochet hook, ch 5 sts, sl
st into 1st ch to form a loop.

Point Ch 3, sc into 2nd ch from hook, hdc in
last ch, sc into ring.

Repeat this 4 more times to make 5 points.

Fasten off.

ALTERNATIVE FLOWER EMBELLISHMENTS

Using E4 (3.50mm) crochet hook, ch 5 sts, sl st into 1st ch
to form a loop.

Next round Ch 2, sc 15 sts into the loop, sl st in to 2nd ch.

Next round *Ch 3, miss 1 sc, sl st into next sc, ch 3, miss 1
   sc; rep from * to end of round, sl st into 1st ch. (5 loops.)

Next round Sc 1, hdc 3, sc 1 into each loop.

Fasten off.

Festive footwork

Celebrate the festive season in unique style by knitting up your own decorations. Here we feature a candy-striped Christmas stocking to hang by the fireplace ready for Santa's visit, and some cute mini-socks for a special sock-themed advent calendar.

Measurements

After fulling, the stocking is approximately 16in (40cm) long from cuff to heel and 12in (30cm) from heel to toe

Gather together...

MATERIALS
A 4 x 3½oz (100g) balls of super bulky-weight (super-chunky) wool yarn in rose pink
B 2 x 3½oz (100g) balls of super bulky-weight (super-chunky) wool yarn in candy pink

NEEDLES AND NOTIONS
1 pair of size 15 (10mm) needles

Gauge

Before fulling: 7 sts and 9 rows to 4in (10cm) measured over st st using size 15 (10mm) needles

Special instruction

Note that the definition between the darker garter stitch stripes and lighter stockinette is lost once fulled, as the process shrinks the fabric, and the knitted fibres mesh together to create a thick, dense fabric that looks and feels like felt.

Knit your stocking...

Using size 15 (10mm) needles and yarn A, cast on 14 sts.
Row 1 K.
Row 2 K1, kfb, k to last 2 sts, kfb, k1.
Rep rows 1 and 2 a further 3 times. 22 sts.

*Change to yarn B
Row 9 K1, kfb, k to last 3 sts, k2tog, k1.
Row 10 P.
Row 11 K.
Row 12 P.
Rep rows 9 to 12 once more.

Change to yarn A
Row 17 As row 9.
Rows 18 to 20 K.
Rep rows 17 to 20 once more.*

Rep from * to * once more, then rep rows 9 to 16 again.

SHAPE REST OF STOCKING

Using yarn A, cast on 44 sts on to the needle with the foot sts. 66 sts.
Next row K across all 44 sts and across foot sts to last 3 sts, k2tog, k1. 65 sts.
K 3 rows.
Next row K to last 3 sts, k2tog, k1. 64 sts.
K 3 rows.

Change to yarn B.
Next row K to last 3 sts, k2tog, k1. 63 sts.
Next row P.
Next row K.
Next row P.
Rep last 4 rows once more. 62 sts.

Change to yarn A.
Next row K to last 3 sts, k2tog, k1. 61 sts.
K 3 rows.
Rep last 4 rows once more. 60 sts.

Father Christmas won't be the only person to appreciate these hand-knitted decorations! Use your stitching skills to create some festive fun in your home, with a sock-themed advent calendar full of tiny treats (see page 123), and a sturdy striped stocking ready for the larger gifts.

SHAPE HEEL AND CREATE FOLD

Change to yarn B.

Next row K to last 3 sts, k2tog, k1. 59 sts.

Next row P.

Rep last 2 rows 3 more times. 56 sts.

Next row K.

Next row P.

Next row K to last 2 sts, kfb, k1. 57 sts.

Next row P.

Rep last 2 rows 3 more times. 60 sts.

Change to yarn A.

K 3 rows.

Next row K to last 2 sts, kfb, k1. 61 sts.

Rep last 4 rows once more. 62 sts.

Change to yarn B.

Next row K.

Next row P.

Next row K.

Next row P1, pfb, p to end. 63 sts.

Rep last 4 rows once more. 64 sts.

Change to yarn A.

K 3 rows.

Next row K1, kfb, k to end. 65 sts.

Rep last 4 rows once more. 66 sts.

Bind off 44 sts (22 sts rem).

Rejoin yarn B and k to end.

Next row P.

Next row K.

Next row P1, pfb to last 2 sts, p2tog, k1.

Next row K.

Next row P.

Next row K.

Next row P1, pfb to last 2 sts, p2tog, k1.

**Change to yarn A.

K 3 rows.

Next row K1, kfb, k to last 3 sts, k2tog.

Rep last 4 rows once.

Change to yarn B.

Next row K.

Next row P.

Next row K.

Next row P1, pfb to last 2 sts, p2tog, k1.

Rep last 4 rows once more.**

Work from ** to ** once.

Rejoin yarn A.

Next row K.

Next row K1, k2tog, k to last 3 sts, k2tog, k1. 64 sts.

Rep last 2 rows 3 more times. 58 sts.

Next row K.

Bind off.

TOP OF STOCKING

With wrong side facing, pick up and knit 60 sts across top of stocking.

Knit every row for 32 rows.

Bind off.

Making up

Darn in any loose ends.

Fold stocking over with right sides facing and join edges.

Turn right side out, fold over stocking top and sew cast-on edge to stocking.

Now full in washing machine set to 50 degrees. Pull into shape while still wet and dry flat.

Mini socks

These miniature socks will make a fun addition to your Christmas decorations. Tuck a tiny treat into each one to enjoy in the countdown to Christmas.

Measurements

Approximately 4½in (11.5cm) long from cuff to heel.

Gather together...

MATERIALS

Oddments of light-weight (DK) yarn in shades of red, green and cream.

NEEDLES AND NOTIONS

1 set of size 4 (3.5mm) double-pointed needles

Stitch marker

Gauge

Achieving an exact gauge is not essential for this project.

Seasonal stripes

For our lively striped pattern, work as for main sock pattern, casting on with main colour yarn. On complete rounds between * and * change to second colour and work 2 rounds of each colour until **. Change to main colour to work heel. Then cont stripe pattern between *** and ***. Change to main colour again to work toe.

Number each sock for the advent calendar from 1 to 24. We used large beads and number transfers to do this. To hang the socks up, crochet a chain as long as the area where you'll be hanging them, then attach the socks at even intervals.

Knit your advent socks

(**Work 24 socks**; one for each day on the advent calendar)

Using size 4 (3.5mm) double-pointed needles, cast on 20 sts. Distribute sts evenly over 3 needles, placing a stitch marker to denote beg of round.

Work 6 rounds in k1, p1 rib.

K 18 rounds.

HEEL FLAP

Divide sts onto 2 needles so that there are 10 sts on each.

**Working on just 1 set of sts, work 15 rows in st st, slipping the 1st st of every row.

SHAPE HEEL

With RS facing, sl 1, k5, ssk, turn.

Next row Sl 1, p2, p2tog, turn.

Next row Sl 1, k2, ssk, turn.

Next row Sl 1, p2, p2tog, turn.

Next row Sl 1, k2, ssk, turn.

Next row Sl 1, p2, p2tog, turn. 4 sts rem.

K2 sts.

GUSSET

Needle 1 K2, pick up and knit 8 sts.

Needle 2 K10.

Needle 3 Pick up and knit 8 sts, k2 sts from heel flap. 30 sts.

SHAPE GUSSET

Round 1

Needle 1 K to last 3 sts, k2tog, k1.

Needle 2 K.

Needle 3 k1, ssk, k to end.

Round 2

K all 3 needles.

Rep last 2 rounds until 20 sts rem.**

FOOT

K14 rounds.

SHAPE TOE

****Round 1

Needle 1 K2, k2tog, k1.

Needle 2 K1, ssk, k to last 3 sts, k2tog, k1.

Needle 3 K1, ssk, k2.

Round 2

Needle 1 K1, k2tog, k1.

Needle 2 K1, ssk, k to last 3 sts, k2tog, k1.

Needle 3 K1, ssk, k1.

Round 3

Needle 1 K2tog, k1.

Needle 2 K1, ssk, k2tog, k1.

Needle 3 K1, ssk and k2 sts on needle 1.

Turn sock right side out and graft toe (see page 21).****

Heels and toes

For a striking alternative, knit your socks in one colour with a contrast colour cuff, heel and toe. Work as for main sock pattern, working the ribbed cuff in a contrast colour yarn, then working the rest in the main fabric but changing to a contrast colour for the heel, changing back to the main colour yarn again and then changing again for the toe.

Charts

Here are the charts you'll need to make the Tiger Feet (pages 82–84) and the Fairy Socks (pages 90–93).

Chart for tiger-feet bootees

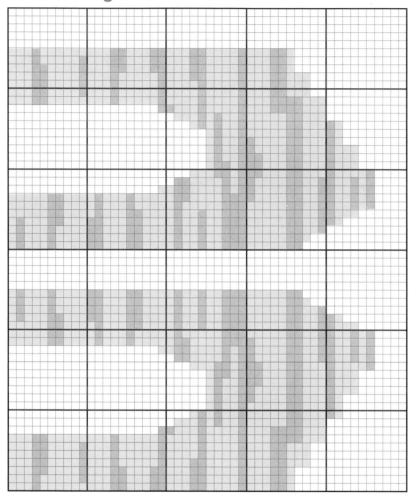

Chart for Fairy socks

CHART A: RIGHT SOCK
NB: The chart is knitted from the top down.

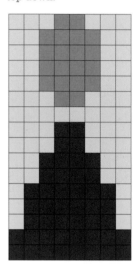

CHART B: LEFT SOCK
NB: The chart is knitted from the top down.

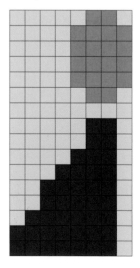

☐ Yarn D

■ Yarn B

☐ Yarn A

☐ Yarn C

Acknowledgments

Lou dedicates her patterns in this book to the memory of her mum Anita Wells, who helped decide on some of the designs before she died. Without her, Lou would never have discovered the wonderful crafts of knitting and crocheting. Lou carries Anita's amazing strength as a great inspiration to all she does.

Kirstie gives big love and thanks to Mum, Dad and Simon for their time and support while she was working on the book.

The publishers would like to thank Nicola Hodgson for writing and compiling the frontmatter of the book. Thanks also go to Lorna Yabsley and her team for their fantastic work producing the photography.

Suppliers

Use the contact details listed below to source the yarns and embellishments used for the projects in this book.

US

Knitting Fever
315 Bayview Avenue
Amityville
NY 11701
Tel: (516) 546 3600
www.knittingfever.com

Purl
137 Sullivan Street
New York NY 10012
Tel: (212) 420 8796
www.purlsoho.com

Rowan and RYC
Rowan USA
4 Townsend West
Suite 8, Nashua
NH 03063
Tel: (603) 886 5041
www.knitrowan.com

Sirdar USA
Wool-Tyme
2–190 Colonnade Rd S
Ottawa
ON, K2E 7J5
Canada
Tel:1-888-241-7653
www.wool-tyme.com

Yarnmarket, Inc.
12936 Stonecreek Drive
Unit D
Pickerington
OH 43147
Tel: 1-888-996-9276
www.yarnmarket.com

UK

Angel Yarns
Angel House
77 North Street
Portslade
East Sussex
BN41 1DZ
Tel: 0870 766 6212
www.angelyarns.com

Artesano Ltd
28 Mansfield Road
Reading
Berkshire
RG1 6AJ
Tel: 0118 9503350
www.artesanoyarns.co.uk

Colinette Yarns
Units 2–5
Banwy Industrial Estate
Llanfair Caereinion
Powys
SY21 0SG
Tel: 01938 552141
www.colinette.com

Debbie Cripps
8 Christchurch Street
West Frome
Somerset
BA11 1EQ
Tel: 01373 454448
www.debbiecripps.co.uk

Designer Yarns
Unit 8–10
Newbridge Industrial Estate
Pitt Street
Keighley
West Yorkshire
BD21 4PQ
Tel: 01535 664222
www.designeryarns.uk.com

English Yarns
19 East Street
Shoreham-by-Sea
West Sussex
BN43 5ZE
Tel: 01273 461029
www.englishyarns.co.uk

Get Knitted
39 Brislington Hill
Brislington
Bristol
BS4 5BE
Tel: 0117 300 5211
www.getknitted.com

Laughing Hens
Southover Nurseries
Spring Lane
Burwash
East Sussex
TN19 7JB
Tel: 01435 883777
www.laughinghens.com

Rowan and RYC
Green Lane Mill
Holmfirth
West Yorkshire
HD9 2DX
Tel: 01484 681881
www.knitrowan.com
www.ryclassic.com

Texere Yarns
College Mill
Barkerend Road
Bradford
West Yorkshire
BD1 4AU
Tel: 01274 722191
www.texere.co.uk

Twilleys of Stamford
Roman Mill
Little Casterton Road
Stamford
Lincs
PE9 1BG
Tel: 01780 752661
www.twilleys.co.uk

Yarns details

Here we have listed the exact brands and shades of yarns used to create the projects.

PAGES 28–31 FIRST STEP TUBE SOCKS

Patons Diploma Gold DK (55% wool, 25% acrylic, 20% nylon – 131yd/120m per ball)

Raspberry Ribbing
2 x 1¾oz (50g) ball of 06129 (Berry)

Tutti Frutti Bands
A 1 x 1¾oz (50g) ball of 06240 (Lupin)
B 1 x 1¾oz (50g) ball of 06129 (Berry)
C 1 x 1¾oz (50g) ball of 06158 (Hollyhock)
D 1 x 1¾oz (50g) ball of 06222 (Lemon)

Lemon 'n' Lime
1 x 1¾oz (50g) ball of 06125 (Apple Green)
1 x 1¾oz (50g) ball of 06222 (Lemon)

PAGES 32–33 TWO-STRIPE TWO-NEEDLE SOCKS

A 1 x 1¾oz (50g) ball of Patons Diploma Gold DK (55% wool, 25% acrylic, 20% nylon – 131yd/120m per ball) in 06129 (Berry)
B 1 x 3½oz (100g) ball of Sirdar Bonus DK (100% acrylic – 306yd/280m per ball) in 930 (Tangerine)

PAGES 34–39 OFF THE CUFF SOCKS

Patons Diploma Gold DK (55% wool, 25% acrylic, 20% nylon – 131yd/120m per ball)

All in Jest

A 2 [2: 3] x 1¾oz (50g) balls in 06171 (Delphinium)
B 1 [1: 1] x 1¾oz (50g) ball in 06123 (Cyclamen)

Going Loopy
2 [2: 3] x 1¾oz (50g) balls in 06123 (Cyclamen)

Fabulous Furry Socks
2 x 1¾oz (50g) balls in 06242 (Violet)
1 x 1¾oz (50g) ball of Patons Whisper Gem (100% polyester – 98yd/90m per ball) in 0020 (Lilac)

PAGES 40–45 A LITTLE EXTRA TOUCH

Celtic Cables
2 x 3½oz (100g) balls of Elle Mexican Wave DK (100% acrylic – 328yd/300m per ball) in 058 (Blue Rush)

Peppermint Pompoms
2 [2: 3] x 1¾oz (50g) balls of Patons Fairytale DK (60% acrylic, 40% nylon – 160yd/147m per ball) in 06304 (Peppermint)

PAGES 46–49 LINGERIE LACE STOCKINGS

Main colourway
5 x 1¾oz (50g) balls of RYC Silk Wool DK (50% merino wool, 50% silk – 109yd/100m per ball) in 307 (Velvet)

Luxury Knee-Highs
4 x 1¾oz (50g) balls of RYC Baby Alpaca DK (100% baby alpaca – 109yd/100m per ball) in 202 (Thistle)

PAGES 50–53 RIDING THE WAVE SOCKS

Main colourway
Debbie Bliss Pure Cashmere (100% cashmere – 49yd/45m per ball)
A 3 x ⅞oz (25g) skeins in 05

B 1 x ⅞oz (25g) skeins in 04

Monochrome Magic
Debbie Bliss Cashmerino Aran (12% cashmere, 55% merino wool, 33% microfibre – 98yd/90m per ball)
A 2 x 1¾oz (50g) balls in 300 (Black)
B 1 x 1¾oz (50g) ball in 101 (Off White)

PAGES 54–57 SHORT AND SWEET SOCKETTES

2 x 1¾oz (50g) balls of Sublime Angora Merino DK (80% extra-fine merino wool, 20% angora – 131yd/120m per ball) in 41 (Cream)
or 2 x 1¾oz (50g) balls of Debbie Bliss Alpaca Silk DK (80% alpaca, 20% silk – 115yd/105m per ball) in 17

PAGES 60–63 BALLERINA BLISS SLIPPERS

Sirdar Bonus DK (100% acrylic – 306yd/280m per ball)

Main colourway
1 x 3½oz (100g) ball in 944 (Cupid)

Embroidered version
1 x 3½oz (100g) ball in 978 (Sunflower)

Buttons version
1 x 3½oz (100g) ball in 998 (Turquoise)

Beaded version
1 x 3½oz (100g) ball in 985 (Violet)

PAGES 64–69 SNOWFLAKE SPECIALS

Swedish Felted Slippers
5 x 1¾oz (50g) balls of Patons Jet (70% wool, 30% alpaca – 81yd/74m per ball) in 706 (Red)
Oddment of light-weight (DK) wool in cream. If you don't have an appropriate oddment in your stash, you could buy a tapestry yarn rather than a full ball of wool.

Winter Wonderland Socks

3 x 1¾oz (50g) balls of Patons Jet (70% wool, 30% alpaca – 81yd/74m per ball) in 706 (Red)

Oddment of light-weight (DK) wool in cream. If you don't have an appropriate oddment in your stash, you could buy a tapestry yarn rather than a full ball of wool.

PAGES 70–73 GORILLA FEET SLIPPERS

A 1 x 1¾oz (50g) ball of Debbie Bliss Cashmerino Aran (55% merino wool, 33% microfibre, 12% cashmere – 98yd/90m per ball) in 300 (Black)

B 3 x 1¾oz (50g) balls of Sirdar Foxy Fur (100% polyester – 44yd/40m per ball) in 432 (Arctic Fox)

PAGES 74–79 SLEEPING PARTNERS

Sublime Angora Merino DK (80% extra-fine merino wool, 20% angora – 131yd/120m per ball)

Curly Cuff Bedsocks

2 x 1¾oz (50g) balls in 44 (Lilac)

Seed Stitch Softie

4 x 1¾oz (50g) balls in 44 (Lilac)

PAGES 82–85 SUPER-CUTIE BOOTEES

Patons Diploma Gold DK (55% wool, 25% acrylic, 20% nylon – 131yd/120m per ball)

Tiger Feet

A 1 x 1¾oz (50g) ball in 06183 (Black)

B 1 x 1¾oz (50g) ball in 06228 (Honey)

Strawberry Shortbread

A 1 x 1¾oz (50g) ball in 06151 (Red)

B 1 x 1¾oz (50g) ball in 06125 (Apple Green)

C 1 x 1¾oz (50g) ball in 06228 (Honey)

Ladybug Spots

A 1 x 1¾oz (50g) ball in 06183 (Black)

B 1 x 1¾oz (50g) ball in 06151 (Red)

PAGES 86–89 DRESSING-UP SOCKS

Ballet Shoes

A 2 x 1¾oz (50g) balls of Sublime Extra Fine Merino Wool DK (100% extra fine merino wool – 126yd/116m per ball) in 05

(Milk)

B 1 x 1¾oz (50g) ball of Sirdar Snowflake DK (100% polyester – 185yd/169m per ball) in 212 (Petal Pink)

Soccer Boots

Sublime Extra Fine Merino Wool DK (100% extra fine merino wool – 126yd/116m per ball)

A 2 x 1¾oz (50g) balls in 05 (Milk)

B 1 x 1¾oz (50g) balls in 07 (Sailor)

Oddment of black yarn for embellishment

PAGES 90–93 FAIRY SOCKS

Rowan 4ply Soft (100% merino wool – 191yd/175m per ball)

A 1 x 1¾oz (50g) ball in 370 (Whisper)

B 1 x 1¾oz (50g) ball in 401 (Tea Rose)

C 1 x 1¾oz (50g) ball in 395 (Fairy)

D 1 x 1¾oz (50g) ball in 367 (Leafy)

E 1 x 1¾oz (50g) ball in 376 (Nippy)

PAGES 94–97 SECRET-KEEPER SOCKS

Jungle Explorer Socks

Patons Jet (30% alpaca, 70% wool – 80yd/74m per ball)

A 2 x 1¾oz (50g) balls in 5 (Brown Navy)

B 1 x 1¾oz (50g) ball in 502 (Chartreuse)

Pink Pockets

Rowan Pure Wool DK (100% super-wash wool – 137yd/125m per ball)

A 2 x 1¾oz (50g) balls in 025 (Tea Rose)

B 1 x 1¾oz (50g) ball in 039 (Lavender)

PAGES 98–99 PIRATE SOCKS

Sirdar Bonus DK (100% acrylic – 306yd/280m per ball)

A 1 x 3½oz (100g) ball in 977 (Signal Red)

B 1 x 3½oz (100g) ball in 965 (Black)

PAGES 102–105 PEEP-TOE PEDICURE SOCKS

Main colourway

1 x 5¼oz (150g) hank of Hummingbird by Artesano Alpaca (100% pure alpaca – 327yd/300m per hank) in 860 (Woodpecker)

Citrus Blocks

Bergere de France Ideal (40% worsted wool, 30% acrylic, 30% polyamide – 137yd/125m per ball)

2 x 1¾oz (50g) balls of 241.091 (Vitamine)

1 x 1¾oz (50g) ball of 225.241 (Chartreuse)

PAGES 106–109 FIVE-TOE STRIPY SOCKS

Sirdar Denim Tweed DK (60% acrylic, 25% cotton, 15% wool – 185yd/170m per ball)

A 1 x 1¾oz (50g) ball in 649 (Nutmeg)

B 1 x 1¾oz (50g) ball in 509 (Beige)

C 1 x 1¾oz (50g) ball in 502 (Denim Blue)

PAGES 110–115 LUSCIOUS LEGWARMERS

Loveheart Legwarmers

2 x 3½oz (100g) balls of Rowan Scottish Tweed Aran (100% pure new wool – 186yd/170m per ball) in 024 (Porridge)

Bell-Bottomed Beauties

2 x 1¾oz (50g) balls of Noro Silk Garden (45% silk, 45% kid mohair, 10% lambswool – 110yd/100m per ball) in 224

PAGES 116–119 SILKY SPLIT-TOE SOCKS

Sirdar Baby Bamboo (80% bamboo, 20% wool – 105yd/96m per ball)

2 x 1¾oz (50g) balls in 134 (Babe) for main sock

Oddments for embellishments in 133 (Willow), 138 (Waterbaby), 139 (Ming), 140 (Minky) and 137 (Little Lilac)

PAGES 120–123 FESTIVE FOOTWORK

Stocking

Rowan Big Wool (100% wool – 87yd/80m per ball)

A 4 x 3½oz (100g) balls in 36 (Glamour)

B 2 x 3½oz (100g) balls in 14 (Whoosh)

Mini Socks

Oddments of light-weight (DK) yarn in shades of red, green and cream

Index